Eat Your Art Out, Chicago
A Guide to Gallery Bars & Restaurants

Ed Sweet
Kimberly Ward

Urbs In Photo, Inc.
Chicago

Cover Illustration:
Mary Flock

Cover Design:
Liska and Associates, Inc.

Title:
Millie Sweet

Interior Design:
Jacqueline Moriarty

Edited by:
Adrienne G. Silverman

Published by:
Urbs In Photo, Inc.
P.O. Box 06236
Sears Tower
Chicago, IL 60606
312/248-1720

ISBN 0-9623419-0-8
ISSN 1044-4335

Copyright © 1989 by Urbs In Photo, Inc.

All rights reserved, including the right to reproduce
this book or any portion thereof in any form.

Extreme care has been taken to see that all information
in this book is accurate and up-to-date, but the publisher
cannot be held responsible for any errors that may appear.

First Edition

Thanks to everyone who made this publication possible,
especially Millie, Francis, Rita, Tom & Michael

Table of Contents

Introduction x

How to Use This Book xiv

Listings 2
   Alchemy Cafe 2
   Alexander's/Cristal 4
   Artful Dodger Pub 6
   At the Tracks 8
   Avalon Niteclub 10
   John Barleycorn Memorial Pub 12
   Batteries Not Included 14
   Bistro Too 16
   Buddies' 18
   Café Coffee 20
   Café on Grand 22
   Cafe Pavo 24
   Café Voltaire 26
   Caffé Pergolesi 28
   Cairo 30
   Charleston 32
   Chris Café 34
   Club Dreamerz 36
   Club 950 Lucky Number 38
   Diva Caffè 40
   The Eccentric 42
   Ennui Café 44

Esoteria	46
Exit	48
F/X 1100	50
Far Side, Inc.	52
Gentry and the Café	54
Grant's Tavern & Grill	56
Guthries Tavern	58
Heartland Cafe, General Store & Buffalo Bar	60
Izimbra	62
Java Jive	64
Jean Claude	66
Jerome's	68
The Lizard Lounge	70
The Local Option	72
Lounge Ax	74
Maxtavern	76
Medici Gallery and Coffee House	78
Medusa's	80
No Exit Café-Gallery	82
Northside Cafe	84
Not Just Pasta	86
Outtakes	88
Pastafina	90
Phyllis' Musical Inn	92
Printer's Row	94
The Rainbo Club	96
River North Café	98
Roscoe's Tavern	100

Savories	102
Sheffield's/School Street Café	104
Star Top Café	106
Sterch's	108
Sweet Home Chicago	110
The 3rd Coast (on Dearborn)	112
The 3rd Coast (on Wabash)	114
Traffic Jam	116
Trio	118
Union	120
Urbus Orbis	122
Vegetaria Restaurant	124
Wholesome Roc Gallery	126
Wild Onion	128
The Wrightwood Tap	130

Introduction

Eat Your Art Out, Chicago features more than 60 local eating and drinking establishments that exhibit and sell artwork. While they may seem unlikely outlets for artistic expression, these restaurants and bars reflect a growing trend in Chicago's artistic community. The increasing number of these venues as alternative art spaces has broadened the city's viewing and buying audience. Displaying art where eating, drinking and conversing co-exist brings art out of isolation from the society it investigates and throws it into the pot-luck mix of life.

A large part of this gallery bar and restaurant movement is the recent revival of the coffee house in Chicago. Traditionally, coffee houses have been fertile ground for brewing revolutionary ideas in art, science and politics. For example, it was in the Café Guerbois and similar coffee houses in Paris that Claude Monet, Édouard Manet, Pierre-Auguste Renoir, Paul Cézanne and other artists discussed their work and the theories that led to the development of modern painting. In recent years, the coffee house has been less influential; however, it still maintains its status as a nurturer of new ideas and forms of expression.

In Chicago, **Caffé Pergolesi** has been such a place for the past 22 years. **The 3rd Coast**, **Diva Caffè** and **Urbus Orbis**--relatively new coffee houses--show the work of local artists to establish neighborhood roots and stimulate dynamic dialog. **Java Jive**, also new, has tailored its interior for exhibits, thus making artwork the dominant feature.

The fact that so many bars and restaurants include art as a component of their entertainment mix is a response to a renewed and more public interest in art. The trend also is a commentary on the distorted power of the formal gallery--the notion that art can only be appreciated in a pristine, white room. Branching out into alternative spaces is part of the progression that has defined the history of a volatile art world. This gallery bar and restaurant movement is of the same stuff that first brought art into private galleries when government-regulated viewing became too restrictive.

Historically, in France the only public art exhibition was the annual show of the French Royal Academy of Painting and Sculpture--the Salon--sponsored by the government from 1667 to 1881. During the 19th Century, progressive artists like Manet and Cézanne, rejected by the official Salon, established alternative exhibitions in order to get exposure. One of the most important was the Salon des Refuses, held in Paris in 1863. The renegade exhibition succeeded in undermining the authority of the official Salon and paved the way for other artists to organize their own independent shows. The importance of art dealers was likewise increased in the more open climate.

The galleries we know today evolved from the bold actions of artists in 19th Century France. Like the Salon, the gallery has become the established art source in a world that views art as a commodity. Artists and collectors are part of a community that has seen record dollars for works by famous living and deceased artists. The media attention generated from these sums has created an ever-growing appetite for art by the masses.

But galleries have become increasingly cautious under pressure to sell work produced by an elite group of artists. This poses a problem for the many artists that are unable to break into the gallery world.

Bars and restaurants that exhibit artwork provide a viable solution. Since these establishments don't depend on art sales for their livelihoods, they are more willing to show experimental work and can afford to take chances on unknowns. The dynamic atmosphere of these new alternative spaces may result in the production of future masterpieces.

The art world is no longer restricted by venue, form or finance. As the barriers of how art is defined are broken down, so are the notions of where art can be viewed. For many Chicago and Midwestern artists, exhibiting work in bars and restaurants has become an alternative to showing in galleries. **Wholesome Roc Gallery** was created to combat restrictive requirements of many galleries too concerned with sales. **Outtakes** gives photographers much needed space to show their work.

This new breed of bars, restaurants, coffee houses and dance clubs exhibits the work of various artists from a range of backgrounds in support of a burgeoning art community. In turn, these alternative spaces benefit from the interest, the atmosphere and the upfront challenge much of the art generates. The interaction between artist and patron creates an exchange of ideas and reaches a wider audience than just gallery goers. Several bars and restaurants have begun to exhibit works in cooperation with progressive galleries, e.g., **Cairo**, **Wild Onion**, **The Local Option**, **At the Tracks**, and **River North Café**.

There is a belief among many artists that the gallery is merely an elitist enclave. Like Thomas Hart Benton, the noted painter and teacher of

Jackson Pollock, these artists prefer to show their work in a saloon. The important difference between a bar or restaurant that shows art and a gallery is the daily interaction of art and real life. Henri Matisse believed art should be that which makes life a pleasure. He sought to fill the gap between art and life. *Eat Your Art Out, Chicago* seeks to expose those outlets that continue this quest.

How to Use This Book

Eat Your Art Out, Chicago is for artists, art collectors and dealers, restaurateurs and bar owners, tourists and anyone interested in eating and drinking in Chicago's hottest bars, restaurants, coffee houses and dance clubs. These venues range from neighborhood taverns to formal dining rooms and represent the entire city. The sole criterion is the establishment's active interest in showing art. Most are concentrated in the Lincoln Park, River North, Lakeview, Wicker Park and Bucktown districts on Chicago's North Side and Hyde Park on the South Side.

Each entry is listed alphabetically and set up on two facing pages. The left-hand side gives the name of the establishment; its classification, location, phone number and hours of operation; who to contact about art exhibits; the frequency of exhibit rotation; and the types and forms of artwork shown. Following this thumbnail sketch is a general description of each establishment's atmosphere, with information about clientele, special nights, cover charges and dinner prices. It's a great dining and nightlife guide for natives and tourists alike.

The right-hand page offers information about why each establishment includes artwork as part of its environment. Restaurants and bars benefit from the decor changes these shows create, as well as from the business generated by regular patrons who look forward to the exhibits and the friends and families of each artist with work on the walls.

There also is information for artists about exhibiting at each establishment. This section is broken down into six parts. The first covers how each establishment reviews proposed shows. The second discusses the installation of artwork, including space available and the use of hardware. The third part explains the insurance provisions of each establishment, while the fourth treats the selling of artwork, including the collection of money and commissions taken. Opening receptions are discussed in the fifth part, with information about scheduling and special arrangements. Part six surveys promotion, including the availability of mailing lists, advertising and on-site publicity.

Many establishments get involved to ensure a successful show experience for artists. Others simply provide wall space and stay out of the planning and execution of exhibits. Reading *Eat Your Art Out, Chicago* and going to the various establishments will help artists find the right places to show their work.

The information in this book also is valuable to art collectors and gallery owners looking for the next hot artists. Several of the establishments in this book claim to have launched the careers of various artists. The work displayed in bars and restaurants is often innovative and exciting, and is usually priced in the $50-500 range.

Restaurants and bars can benefit from *Eat Your Art Out, Chicago* by learning from the experts. Seeing how other establishments have exhibited art to their benefit can help in refining or developing systems for showing work.

Whatever your perspective, *Eat Your Art Out, Chicago* offers a feast of information on how to get involved in one of the most appetizing art movements to come around in a long time. Bon appetit!

The following outlines the format of each entry given in this book:

Name of establishment
Classification (Type of establishment, cuisine and/or musical emphasis)

Street address
Phone number
Hours of operation

Art contact
Frequency of exhibit rotation
Type of work exhibited (Most places exhibit wall hangings of all kinds. A few limit themselves to specific types, e.g., photographs. Establishments that accept a variety of art forms, including sculpture, are listed as Unrestricted)

Description of establishment (Atmosphere, clientele, type of food, special nights, cover charges and dinner prices)

Art Philosophy (Reasons establishment exhibits artwork)

Exhibiting (A step-by-step guide to exhibition requirements)

Alchemy Cafe
American

1835 W. North Avenue
Chicago, IL 60622
312/276-4448
Tue.-Thurs., 4 p.m.-10 p.m.; Fri.-Sat., 4 p.m.-11 p.m.

Diane Celia Rosen, Owner
Indefinite
Wall Hangings

Alchemy Cafe offers a richness in food and atmosphere. The dinners are large meals one would normally have at home, like chicken & dumplings and baked macaroni & cheese. Like the alchemist who attempted to turn base metals into gold, Alchemy Cafe succeeds in turning raw ingredients into something more valuable. The a la carte menu changes every week. Expect to pay $25 per couple for dinner.

The large room is as inviting as a comfortable home. A high, tin ceiling is painted a rich burgundy, matched by a set of softly spinning ceiling fans. The light is warm and low, complementing the cream-colored walls. A light blue railing stretches around the room at waist height, and the walls just below are a deep midnight blue. Rectangular tables are covered with striking fabrics--some patterned, some solid. Dark wooden chairs surround each table and accommodate a clientele of students, professionals and artists.

Art Philosophy

Alchemy Cafe hopes to make art accessible and provide a unique interaction among art, space, food and humanity. Many people feel intimidated by galleries and gallery openings, but exhibits at the café make art a part of everyday life.

Exhibiting

Make an appointment to present slides or original pieces for review. Most important is to like the atmosphere, want to show there, and want to share art with people who would not otherwise see it. Group shows OK.

Artist handles installation. There are two available walls, measuring 12-1/2' by 8' and 14' by 8'.

Artist is responsible for insurance.

Artwork is purchased by contacting the artist directly. Alchemy Cafe does not take a commission.

Openings are held on Mondays and are arranged on an individual basis.

Alchemy Cafe will promote exhibits in normal mailings. Inside the restaurant, the artist may post a price list, bio and title cards next to each piece.

Alexander's/Cristal
American/Jazz

217 W. Huron Street
Chicago, IL 60610
312/951-8151
Daily, 5 p.m.-4 a.m.

Bruce Kaufman, Manager
Indefinite
Unrestricted

Upstyle and Euro-chic, Alexander's is splashed with hot pink and furnished with zebra-skin booths and high-backed chairs. The chairs, stately thrones around large square tables draped with white linen, command attention in the center of the room, while the deep horseshoe booths lend themselves to more secluded dining. A less formal atmosphere is created outdoors under a pink canopy.

The food at Alexander's is heavy with spices and the portions are generous. The restaurant offers a selection of steaks, seafood and chicken dishes. Expect to pay about $70 per couple for dinner.

Cristal stands in stark contrast to Alexander's. The club, which offers live jazz, fashion shows and dancing, recalls a long-gone Medieval era. It is a fantastical menagerie of stone lions, gargoyles and angels. Chandeliers on the vaulted ceiling are carefully wrapped in white cloth--the atmosphere is lofty and elegant. Cover is $5 on Friday and Saturday.

Art Philosophy

Alexander's/Cristal believes there is value in giving exposure to young artists. Exhibiting artwork also is a way to enhance the musical and culinary arts that already distinguish the restaurant and club.

The art at Alexander's/Cristal usually has an international twist. The establishment has hosted parties for the Polish and Italian Consulates, featuring works by artists of each nationality. Cristal also is used to entertain gallery guests after openings.

Exhibiting

Make an appointment to present work for review. Slides are OK, but the club must see original pieces before final approval is granted.

Artist handles installation. Nails OK. An 8' x 12' wall is available near the front entrance, and smaller spaces on pink pillars are scattered throughout Alexander's.

Artist is responsible for insurance, but the establishment is guarded and has an alarm system.

Artwork is purchased by contacting the artist directly. Alexander's/Cristal does not take a commission.

No formal openings.

Alexander's/Cristal might be open to helping artists promote exhibits by placing listings in monthly calendars. Inside the restaurant, no price lists are allowed, just the tasteful and subtle display of the artist's name and phone number.

Artful Dodger Pub
Dance Club

1734 W. Wabansia Avenue
Chicago, IL 60622
312/227-6859
Mon.-Fri., 5 p.m.-2 a.m.; Sat., 8 p.m.-3 a.m.; Sun., 5 p.m.-1 a.m.
(Closed on Sundays during the summer)

Brian Friedler, Owner
Indefinite
Unrestricted

Artful Dodger Pub is a tavern-a-go-go that attracts all ages of artists, professionals, punk rockers and businesspeople. It is a friendly place to associate with people outside one's normal social spectrum.

DJs play a wide variety of music five nights a week, including hits from the 40s & 50s, R&B, progressive dance, cajun and rock 'n' roll. Live bands, scheduled once a month, command a $3-4 cover. There are many special events at Artful Dodger, including Limbo Nights, Tributes to Elvis, R&B Night on Monday and Ladies Night on Tuesday.

Art Philosophy

Artful Dodger Pub exhibits artwork because a good number of its patrons are artists. Providing wall space shows support for a community which is so supportive of the club.

Artful Dodger Pub commissions local artists to design its weekly *Reader* ads.

Exhibiting

Make an appointment to present work for review or schedule a studio visitation. Slides OK. Photographs are discouraged unless they are large.

Artist handles installation after discussion with the bar. Nails are not encouraged.

Artist is responsible for insurance.

Artwork is purchased by contacting the artist directly. Artful Dodger Pub does not take a commission.

Openings are negotiable.

Artist has access to the club mailing list for promotion. Inside the club, the artist can post a price list, bio and title cards next to each piece.

At the Tracks
American/Blues, Jazz, Rock & Comedy

325 N. Jefferson Street
Chicago, IL 60606
312/332-1124
Mon.-Fri., 10 a.m.-2 a.m.; Sat., 10 a.m.-3 a.m.

Carl Berman, Owner
2 Months
Unrestricted

They're not kidding, this place is literally at the tracks, set in the heart of an industrial area. The renovated, bright yellow brick warehouse-turned-restaurant offers fantastic views of Chicago's Downtown and Near North Side.

A bright dining room occupies the lower level of At the Tracks. Although the room is small, the pale brick, light-colored furniture and lofted ceilings give it a spacious feel. At the Tracks serves moderately-priced eclectic American cuisine, consisting largely of seafood, chicken and beef, to a clientele of advertising and marketing executives, engineers, architects and intellectuals. Expect to pay about $40 per couple for dinner. At the Tracks also offers a good business lunch.

Upstairs, while sandwiches and snacks are served, entertainment is the focus. The mood is jazzier, the lighting is lower and one's attention is directed toward a stage in front of the room. The entertainment includes jazz, reggae, rhythm and blues, rock and comedy. The crowd is a mix of young professionals, artists and actors. Cover is $5-6.

Art Philosophy

At the Tracks exhibits artwork and rotates shows in order to add flavor to its atmosphere. The interior of the club offers a tremendous amount of open wall space that calls out for decoration.

Exhibiting

All the art shown in At The Tracks is obtained through Sybill Larney Gallery. There are always two shows, one on each level.

Gallery handles installation. Nails OK. The second floor performance area has a great deal of exposed brick wall space for large pieces. Smaller pieces work best in the dining room.

Gallery is responsible for insurance.

Artwork is purchased by contacting the gallery directly. At The Tracks does not take a commission.

Weekday openings can be held after a show has been up for awhile. At The Tracks will provide free beer and wine plus a buffet.

Both the gallery and the club do a mailing to promote exhibits. At The Tracks also writes a press release about the artist and his or her work. Inside the club, the artist can post a price list and bio as well as distribute information on tables.

Avalon Niteclub
Dance Club

959 W. Belmont
Chicago, IL 60657
312/472-3020
Wed.-Fri., 9 p.m.-2 a.m.; Sat., 9 p.m.-3 a.m.

Tod Brown, Manager
1 Month
Wall Hangings

Avalon Niteclub contributes to the hard-edged excitement of the neighborhood in which it is located. A long flight of stairs leads to a landing where the space divides into three separate rooms. Straight ahead is a large dance room, wildly muraled by local artists. To the right is a door leading into a space where fashion shows are held, and to the left is a long, narrow hallway that opens into a small room with a bar and stage.

The over-all feeling of the Avalon is subcultural. The mood is dark and the regular crowd is intensely clad in black leather.

On Friday and Saturday nights, as many as four live bands can be heard at the Avalon. Wednesday is Heavy Metal Night, and ladies drink free on Thursday. Cover is $3 on Wednesday and Thursday after 10 p.m. and $5 on Friday and Saturday after 9 p.m.

Art Philosophy

Avalon Niteclub is a meeting place for artists. The club hosts numerous special events in support of local musicians, designers, painters and photographers. The art exhibits keep the place interesting and cater to the creative clientele.

Exhibiting

Make an appointment to present photographs or slides for review. An exhibition organizer must represent several artists for a group show.

Installation is handled by the participating artists and Avalon. There are two 6' by 12' walls and one 15' by 12' wall. Nails OK. All pieces must have their own hanging wire.

Artist is responsible for insurance.

Artwork is purchased through Avalon Niteclub, which does not take a commission. The club will hold money for the artist.

Openings are informal and are usually held on Wednesdays or Thursdays from 9 p.m.-11 p.m. Avalon Niteclub may provide drinks for guests, but exact terms are negotiable.

Avalon Niteclub promotes exhibits in the *Reader*. Flyers offering free admission are printed for openings. Inside the club, the artist may place title cards next to each piece.

John Barleycorn Memorial Pub
Tavern

658 W. Belden Avenue
Chicago, IL 60614
312/348-8899
Sun.-Fri., 11 a.m.-2 a.m.; Sat., 11 a.m.-3 a.m.

Manager
1 Month
Wall Hangings, Projected Slides

At first glance, John Barleycorn Memorial Pub looks like just another charming tavern. Take a second look and understand that the place belongs to a somewhat traditional eccentric, if such a classification can be made.

Established in the 1890s, Barleycorn's has a rich history. During Prohibition, the saloon made its living through a close association with a neighboring laundry. Customers took in their wash and then made their way through the store into a secret entrance to the closed saloon. Amazing how many Chicago husbands did laundry in the 1920s.

Today, Barleycorn's maintains an elaborate antique model boat collection. The room is heavy with dark oak tables, brass chandeliers, and billiard-green curtains hooked onto brass rods. The bar, backed by a thick mirror, offers a selection of English beers on tap which accompany a menu of appetizers and gourmet burgers. A row of dart boards lines the front wall next to the bar. What is surprising is the continual slide show projected on two large screens, an art history lesson accompanied by classical music.

Art Philosophy

John Barleycorn Memorial Pub exhibits artwork to keep its atmosphere interesting.

Exhibiting

Make an appointment to present slides or original pieces for review.

Artist and bar work together to install pieces below the ledge displaying the collection of antique boats. Nails OK. Pieces can measure about 2-1/2' by 2', but there also is wall space for four larger pieces. Artist also can display slides from two projectors.

Artist is responsible for insurance.

Artwork is purchased by contacting the artist directly. John Barleycorn Memorial Pub does not take a commission.

Openings are negotiable.

Promotion is the responsibility of the artist. Inside the bar, a price list may be placed next to the work.

Batteries Not Included
Alternative Rock

2201 N. Clybourn Avenue
Chicago, IL 60614
312/348-9529 or 312/427-9920
Daily, 4 p.m.-2 a.m.

Marc Delphonse, Owner
1 Month
Wall Hangings

Word of mouth has made Batteries Not Included a well-known spot among international tourists. The cosmopolitan clientele is a nice mix of artists, musicians and professionals who enjoy the laid-back tempo and tropical feel of the front room.

A pool table bridges the gap to the rear concert area, which stands in stark contrast to the main bar. The large room is dark and undecorated, allowing loud bands and rowdy crowds. Cover is usually $4-5.

Art Philosophy

Batteries Not Included is set up as a space to keep art vital and provide emotional, visionary and thought-provoking images to the public. Perhaps not everyone will like what they see--art has the potential to both add and detract from the atmosphere-- but any reaction is better than none at all.

Batteries Not Included seeks art with a message. The bar is eager to feature new young artists who are trying to convey social meaning through their work. Such work is not always commercial and suits the bar's relaxed and intellectual consciousness.

Exhibiting

Bring in original pieces for review and be able to explain what they mean so the bar can recount their stories to inquiring patrons.

Installation is the artist's responsibility. No nails. Available spaces are scattered throughout the front room, mainly near the entrance and by the pool table. Pieces no larger than 3' square work best. The bar will not allow pieces in the back room or in the restrooms due to the potential for damage.

Artist is responsible for insurance. The bar has an alarm system, and the bartenders are able to keep an eye on the pieces.

Artwork is purchased through terms arranged by the artist. The bar will collect money only if the patron can take the piece immediately. Otherwise, the bar will give out the artist's phone number. Batteries Not Included does not take a commission, but will accept a donation from the artist at the end of the show.

Openings are negotiable.

Batteries Not Included does not have a mailing list available, and leaves exhibit promotion to the artist. Inside the bar, promotional pieces are allowed at artist's discretion.

Bistro Too
Dance Club

5015 N. Clark Street
Chicago, IL 60640
312/728-0050
Wed.-Sat., 9 p.m.-4 a.m.

T.L. Noble, Manager & Chuck Renslow, Owner
Up to 2 Months
Unrestricted

High energy and rowdiness define Bistro Too, a dance club catering to a well mixed crowd of lesbians, gays and straights. The Top 40, urban contemporary music is loud and continuous, and the large dance floor is always full.

Bistro Too offers a series of special nights far beyond the typical selection of Ladies Nights and Open Mikes. On Wednesday, one can enjoy Drag Queen Wrestling and the Female Imposters. The Chicago Meatpackers perform an all-male strip show on weekends. Cover is $2 every night but Thursday, when it, and drink prices, are $1.

Art Philosophy

Bistro Too exhibits artwork in order to change its ambiance and give exposure to artists.

The art at Bistro Too tends toward the outlandish, wild, avant garde, sculptural and unusual.

Exhibiting

Make an appointment to present slides or a portfolio for review. Group shows OK.

Installation is handled by the artist and club. Bistro Too has final say over placement of pieces. Nails OK. Most art is shown on the upper level, but a few spaces are available in the foyer.

Artist is responsible for insurance.

Artwork is purchased by contacting the artist directly or through the club. Bistro Too does not take a commission, but will accept a piece as thanks or negotiate a reduced rate.

Openings are negotiable.

Bistro Too will make its mailing list available to the artist. If the artist prints brochures to the club's mailing specifications, the club will do the mailing. Inside the club, the artist can put title cards next to each piece and leave information at the bar.

Buddies'
Tavern/Southwestern

3301 N. Clark Street
Chicago, IL 60657
312/477-4066
Restaurant: Daily, 11 a.m.-Midnight
Bar: Sun.-Fri., 11 a.m.-2 a.m.; Sat., 11 a.m.-3 a.m.

Michael, Manager
2-1/2 Weeks
Wall Hangings

Buddies' draws an upscale crowd to its small, festive dining room. The tables are close together and the noise level is high. The clientele is a split between young urban straights and gays, mostly from the neighborhood. Buddies' menu offers a variety of Southwestern homestyle dishes and daily specials. Expect to pay about $35 per couple for dinner.

The Cheyenne Bar next door is about 75 percent gay, mostly men, and fills up with a vocal crowd of regulars who interact with the employees and management on a personal level. It's a relaxing but boisterous and fun environment with a pool table, arcade games and loud music.

Art Philosophy

Rotating exhibits fit into Buddies' overall interest in keeping things fresh. Even when there isn't a show, spaces in the bar are rearranged and the "permanent" artwork is changed. A new atmosphere helps generate responses from patrons, whose comments tie them more closely to the Buddies' family.

The dining room is more conducive to serious pieces, while the bar's atmosphere invites campy, wild and humorous works.

Exhibiting

Make an appointment to present original pieces for review. Slides are OK if the pieces or the collection are very large, but Buddies' prefers to see at least one original piece. Buddies' will help in selecting a group for display, and requires that all exhibited works be framed.

Buddies' handles installation: artist is not allowed to be present. Pieces are delivered on Wednesday and hung on Thursday. There is space for eight pieces measuring 5' by 4' in the dining area, while smaller pieces work better in the bar. Buddies' is eager to accommodate, and is flexible when it comes to hanging and lighting.

Artist is responsible for insurance, but if the collection is extremely valuable, Buddies' will consider a rider on its policy.

Artwork is purchased by contacting the artist directly. Buddies' will help the artist determine prices. Buddies' does not take a commission, but generally acquires one of the pieces for its own collection.

Openings are held on Thursdays and can run from the traditional wine and cheese reception to a huge White Castle buffet.

Buddies' does all promotion around the shows, in order "to deflate the potential pomposity of the artist." Buddies' sends out flyers using its own mailing list in combination with the artist's. Buddies' encourages the artist to hold publicized office hours to meet customers and discuss the show.

Café Coffee
Coffee House

5211 S. Harper Street
Chicago, IL 60615
312/288-4063
Summer Hours: Mon.-Fri., 10 a.m.-9 p.m.; Sat., 9 a.m.-7 p.m.; Sun., 10 a.m.-6 p.m.
Winter Hours: Mon.-Sat., 9 a.m.-7 p.m.; Sun., 10 a.m.-5 p.m.

David & Pamela Griffin, Co-Owners & Managers
Indefinite
Wall Hangings

Café Coffee is a bright room with tables and chairs scattered on a wooden floor. High stools line a large coffee bar to the left of the entrance. The atmosphere is relaxed, but high energy permeates the space, generated by an animated and mobile clientele of businesspeople, students, artists and tourists.

Café Coffee roasts its own coffee once or twice a week. In the summer, iced coffee made with coffee ice cubes is popular. The coffee house serves sandwiches, quiche and desserts, including scones and a lemon cheese pound cake.

Art Philosophy

Café Coffee exhibits artwork because of the artistic environment in which it is located.

Exhibiting

Make an appointment to present work for review. Slides OK. Café Coffee prefers softer, more traditional drawings, paintings and photographs in favor of bold abstracts.

Artist handles installation. Nails OK. There is a 12' by 10' wall to the right of the entrance and a smaller wall across from the entrance.

Artist is responsible for insurance.

Artwork is purchased by contacting the artist directly or through Café Coffee, which does not take a commission.

Openings are negotiable.

Artist is responsible for promotion. Inside the coffee house, the artist can place title cards next to each piece.

Café on Grand
Café

300 W. Grand Avenue
Chicago, IL 60610
312/321-1140
Mon.-Fri., 8 a.m.-3:30 p.m.; Sat., 10 a.m.-3:30 p.m.

Bob Schwartz, Co-Owner
6 Months +
Black and White Photographs

Café on Grand is a pleasant place to get breakfast or lunch in Chicago's gallery district. The loft space is large, but the atmosphere is warm. The brown, earthy tones of the room play well against the stark white of the tablecloths that provide just enough order and formality.

The café serves coffee, eggs, muffins and fresh sandwiches and salads to area businesspeople, artists and designers from the Merchandise Mart. It is a good starting or finishing point of any morning gallery tour.

Art Philosophy

Café on Grand exhibits the work of local artists to fit in with the surrounding community, provide the café with an inexpensive way to enhance and change its atmosphere, and provide artists with valuable exposure.

Exhibiting

Make an appointment to present original pieces for review. Café on Grand only displays black and white photographs.

Artist handles installation. Nails OK. Prints must be matted to fit into six wooden turquoise-colored frames provided by the café. All frames measure 25" by 21", and may be displayed horizontally or vertically. Each piece is hung above a table along a brick wall.

Artist is responsible for insurance.

Artwork is purchased by contacting the artist directly. Café on Grand does not take a commission.

Openings are negotiable.

Artist is responsible for promotion. The café has no mailing list. Inside the café, the artist can place title cards next to each piece, flyers at the counter, and post a sign near the entrance including a photograph, address and phone number, a statement about the artist's vision or the exhibition itself, and a price list.

Cafe Pavo
Coffee House

3523 N. Clark Street
Chicago, IL 60657
312/975-0304
Mon.-Thurs., Noon-11 p.m.; Fri.-Sat., Noon-1:30 a.m.; Sun., 4 p.m.-11 p.m.

Anne Diaz, Owner
1 Month
Unrestricted

Cafe Pavo gets its name from the Latin word for peacock. Like the bird, the coffee house is splashed with color--bright pinks, reds, greens and blues on painted tables and chairs complement the more subdued colors of the ceiling. The establishment is clean, bright and open, but small enough to be intimate. A section of the main room contains two couches and a coffee table topped with a wide range of magazines. To the left of the entrance is a small gallery with two tables. Stucco walls and large cacti give this room a Southwestern feel.

Don't expect to get a full meal at Cafe Pavo. The place is designed for conversation and relaxation over a cup of coffee. However, the coffee house does serve a small selection of soups, salads, pastries, yoghurt granola and fresh fruit in addition to flavored coffees, teas and juices. The background music ranges among Ella Fitzgerald, Opera, Latin American or Show Tunes. The clientele is a mix of artists, musicians, Rastafarians, professionals, students and Ethiopians.

Cafe Pavo is always looking for new coffee pots to add to its eclectic collection.

Art Philosophy

Cafe Pavo strives to be a place in which to sit, be comfortable and look at and talk about art. Galleries can be intimidating, and the café atmosphere is a nice way to bridge the gap between the public and the art world. Cafe Pavo also is designed for artists who might not be looked at twice at a gallery, so they can benefit from the experience of showing art publicly.

Exhibiting

Make an appointment to present work for review. Original pieces are preferred, but slides are OK. Cafe Pavo is willing and eager to discuss an artist's work, even if a show doesn't happen. Two shows are held simultaneously.

Artist and coffee house handle installation together. Nails OK. In the main room, there is an 18' by 6' wall, two 5' by 6' walls and two 7' by 6' walls. In the gallery, there is a 7' by 10' wall, a 3' by 10' wall and a 12' by 10' wall.

Artist is responsible for insurance and must sign a waiver.

Artwork is purchased through Cafe Pavo, which takes a 10-20 percent commission. Artwork must remain hanging for the duration of the show.

Openings are held on Friday evenings every two weeks. Cafe Pavo will split the cost of wine and hors d'oeuvres with the artist.

Cafe Pavo will split mailing costs for promotion and will tag regular advertising with the fact that art is available at the coffee house. Inside the café, the artist may place information on tables and post a price list, bio and title cards next to each piece.

Café Voltaire
Café

1860 N. Elston Avenue
Chicago, IL 60622
312/489-7792
Mon.-Fri., 6 p.m.-Midnight; Sat.-Sun., 11 a.m.-Midnight

Harry Hoch, Owner
2 Months
Unrestricted

Café Voltaire was inspired by the cabaret in Zurich, Switzerland, Cabaret Voltaire, made famous by its clientele of Dadaist artists such as the painter Arp and the poet Tzara. Like its namesake, Café Voltaire is a haven for innovative artists searching for new means of expression.

The café has many functions. It serves as an informal gathering place, performance space, gallery and coffee house. The rear room is rented out to performance and theatrical groups. Art is placed throughout the large, bright front loft.

The main room resembles a private home. There are comfortable old couches, chairs and tables, lots of books to read, a good selection of music, a pool table and chess boards. The "house pet" is a white gargoyle that consistently occupies its space on the coffee bar in back.

Café Voltaire offers a full menu, largely vegetarian except for a few tuna dishes. The food includes such items as vegetarian sloppy joes, felaffel burgers, pizza, mushroom curry, pastries and, of course, coffee. Cover in the rear room depends on the group renting out the space.

Art Philosophy

Café Voltaire exhibits artwork to expose people to different forms and ideas. The café prefers works that create controversy and stimulate a reaction.

Exhibiting

Make an appointment to present original pieces for review. Slides are OK if the artist has a reputation. Café Voltaire normally hosts group shows.

Artist handles installation. Nails OK. Pieces can be hung on walls, hung from the ceiling, put on the floor or leaned against the wall on top of the book shelves.

Artist is responsible for insurance.

Artwork is purchased at Café Voltaire, which takes a commission.

Openings are held with wine and hors d'oeuvres provided by the café.

Artist is responsible for promotion, but the café may contribute to costs. Inside the café, the artist can post prices next to works and display a bio.

Caffé Pergolesi
Coffee House

3404 N. Halsted Street
Chicago, IL 60657
312/472-8602
Mon.-Thurs., 3 p.m.-1 a.m.; Sun., 9 a.m.-1 a.m.

David Weinberger, Owner & Manager
1 Month-6 Weeks
Wall Hangings

Named after the Italian composer, 22-year-old Caffé Pergolesi is the second-oldest coffee house in Chicago. The dim, intimate atmosphere is conducive to quiet reading, a game of backgammon, or discussions of art, politics and philosophy. The atmosphere is relaxed and casual--not the place to go to if you're in a hurry.

The space is divided into two areas. The front, facing the street, is more social. Board games and newspapers are stacked on ledges for use at the tables, and the conversation can be quite animated. A sign that reads "Buy Art Here" hangs over the entrance to the more private space in the back, where serious group discussions and important planning sessions are held. The service area stands in the middle of the café, providing the required background noise of any good coffee house--the intermittent slurp of the espresso machine.

The clientele is eclectic, made up mostly of young artists, older hippies and neighborhood passers-by. The light menu is strictly vegetarian.

Art Philosophy

Caffé Pergolesi believes art can be better judged in a dynamic, lived-in environment than in a sterile gallery space. Being able to see a piece in a real setting gives the potential buyer a better idea of how the work might fit in at home.

Caffé Pergolesi discourages work that is unduly angry and disturbing, work that is so strong that it cuts into food sales.

Exhibiting

Go to Caffé Pergolesi with a portfolio and an attitude that will convince the management you're serious in the pursuit of well-defined artistic goals. Group shows OK.

Installation is handled jointly. No nails. Ample space is available for several large pieces or many smaller ones. Lighting is dim.

Artist is responsible for insurance.

Artwork is purchased through Caffé Pergolesi, which takes a 30 percent commission. The coffee house is often its own customer.

Openings are held in the rear half of the coffee house from 8 p.m.-1 a.m. on a week night. Coffee may be free. Artist can bring food as long as it is vegetarian.

Caffé Pergolesi generates flyers and news releases to promote exhibits. Inside the coffee house, the "Buy Art Here" sign signals that the works are for sale. Interested patrons may ask the staff for details.

Cairo
Dance Club/American Nouvelle

720 N. Wells Street
Chicago, IL 60610
312/266-6620
Mon.-Thurs., 11:30 a.m.-3 a.m.; Fri., 11:30 a.m-4 a.m.; Sat., 6 p.m.-5 a.m.;
Sun., 9 p.m.-4 a.m.

Page, General Manager
1 Month
Unrestricted

Cairo is a sculptural experience with rich reference to Classical and Modern construction. Palm trees in terra cotta pots stand against plaster supports that widen as they reach the ceiling. Sleek black leather chairs are systematically tucked under white linen-covered tables. A line of narrow Corinthian columns discreetly divides the dining area from the bar and leads to the back of the room where a black piano stands in front of a swooping wall. Behind this wall are stairs leading down to the Dance Club, a dim brick catacombs lit by small candles tucked in natural crevices inside recessed chambers that surround the large dance floor.

Cairo offers a light menu and cocktails in the dining room, accompanied by live jazz Thursday through Sunday. Cover is $5 on Thursday and $7 on weekends. Expect to pay about $50 per couple for dinner. Reservations are accepted, and outdoor seating is available.

On Tuesday, "Cleopatra's Revenge" allows women to drink free champagne from 9 p.m.-Midnight on both levels. Men are charged $3 at the door. On Sunday, dance without a cover from 9 p.m.-4 a.m. Cairo's $125 Gold Card obtains free wine with lunch, instant admission to the Dance Club with one guest, and special private events for cardholders.

Art Philosophy

Cairo enjoys art and the people who enjoy art. The club also has seen the advantage in developing relationships with area galleries, which use the club to extend their wall space and entertain clients.

Exhibiting

Cairo only works with a select group of galleries. An artist off the street may bring in original works for review by the club, which will recommend the artist to the right gallery. Cairo has final say over what is exhibited.

Artist and gallery handle installation. Nails OK. Three bare-brick spaces are available for small hanging pieces in the dining room, usually photographs. A wall framed by a false doorway near the entrance can showcase a painting as large as 5' by 4'. Sculpture may be installed in the outside dining area.

Artist and gallery are responsible for insurance.

Artwork is purchased by contacting the gallery directly. Cairo does not take a commission.

Champagne and hors d'oeuvre openings are held Tuesday nights from 5:30 p.m.-7:30 p.m.

Cairo combines its own 2,600 names with gallery and artist lists for promotion. Cairo designs and distributes announcements and writes press releases. Inside the club, the artist's bio and a price list, provided by the gallery, are posted by the entrance.

Charleston
Tavern

2076 N. Hoyne Avenue
Chicago, IL 60647
312/489-4757
Mon.-Fri., 10 a.m.-2 a.m.; Sat., 10 a.m.-3 a.m.; Sun., Noon-2 a.m.

Wendy Pick, Owner
1 Month
Unrestricted

Charleston is a comfortable meeting place without pretension. Its crowd of artists and musicians mingles comfortably in an atmosphere that is charmingly cluttered and dusty. The bar has a woody, rustic feel. Stuffed animals, real ones, stand guard over the art on the walls. A 100-year-old pool table occupies a solitary position of respect in its own room.

Almost every night is a special one at Charleston. Wednesday is Open Mike, Soviet Discussion Groups are held on the first Monday of each month, and Stupid People Tricks are staged once a month. Live, low-key music is performed every Friday through Sunday with no cover.

Art Philosophy

Charleston is aware that artists need exposure and that it is difficult to break into the gallery world. Providing space can benefit new local talent.

Charleston also benefits from exhibiting artwork. The shows get patrons talking and interacting, and it is interesting to hear the artists in the bar critique the works of their peers.

Exhibiting

Make an appointment to present slides and at least one original piece, if possible, for review. Artist may leave slides with the bartender and wait for a call back.

Artist handles installation. For hanging pieces, the use of picture rails is preferred. Installation takes place on Friday or Saturday. Ample wall space is available for small pieces, but there is room for works as large as 4' by 6'. Sculpture may be placed in the front window.

Artist is responsible for insurance.

Artwork is purchased by contacting the artist directly. Charleston does not take a commission.

Charleston holds formal openings with a piano, sax and flute trio. Drink discounts are negotiable. Artist may bring food.

Charleston promotes exhibits in a Bucktown art newsletter and through its own monthly calendar. The bar will provide the artist with its mailing list. Inside the bar, promotional materials may be displayed at the artist's discretion.

Chris Café
American

201 E. Grand Avenue
Chicago, IL 60611
312/329-1888
Mon.-Sat., 6 a.m.-10 p.m.; Sun., 7 a.m.-3 p.m.

Georgia Xamplas, Manager
Indefinite
Wall Hangings

Chris Café serves an older, professional clientele, although a variety of people come in during the course of a day. The room is clean and bright, colored in blue, white and salmon. White tablecloths rest on tables that line the long, narrow space. Large sheets of white paper are placed on top of the tablecloths, so patrons can sketch and doodle with crayons provided by the restaurant. This customer "art" is often on display at Chris'.

The restaurant offers breakfast, lunch and dinner, with brunch on Saturday and Sunday. Dinner specialties are pasta and fish, but quick, inexpensive sandwiches also are available. Expect to pay between $15-30 per couple for dinner.

Art Philosophy

Chris Café exhibits artwork to enhance its atmosphere.

Exhibiting

Make an appointment to present slides or original pieces for review.

Artist handles installation. Nails OK.

Artist is responsible for insurance.

Artwork is purchased by contacting the artist directly. Chris Café does not take a commission.

No formal openings.

Artist is responsible for promotion. Inside the restaurant, the artist can leave a price list, bio and portfolio of additional work at the counter.

Club Dreamerz
Dance Club

1516 N. Milwaukee Avenue
Chicago, IL 60622
312/252-1155
Sun.-Fri., 8 p.m.-4 a.m.; Sat., 8 p.m.-5 a.m.

Dan Hites, Owner
6 Weeks-2 Months
Mural-Sized Paintings

Club Dreamerz is a place for music and movement. The club attracts a crowd of artists, professionals and new wavers in their mid-to-upper twenties who like to dance and listen to both live and disc jockeyed progressive music.

The main floor holds a long, high-ceilinged bar area with a dance room in the back. Outside is an enclosed beer garden with wild murals painted by local artists. Upstairs, a concert hall packs in about 350 people who are invited to add graffiti to the walls if they can find an open space. Cover upstairs is usually $3-5, but expect to pay in the $10 range for name acts.

Special events include Heavy Metal Night on Monday; Men's Lib Night on Tuesday; International Night on Wednesday, where drinks are free with a passport; and Ladies Night on Thursday.

Art Philosophy

The name Dreamerz is tied into the club's objective of offering a showcase for artists who are just starting out, who have a dream. The club's support of the local artistic community in turn generates good will with the clientele.

Each summer, Dreamerz holds a judged sidewalk chalk-coloring contest for artists that includes an all-day barbecue and cash prizes.

Club Dreamerz seeks new, experimental artists to add color and liveliness to the bar. The club often exhibits work with a sci-fi feel.

Exhibiting

Make an appointment to present work for review. Slides are OK, but a well-presented portfolio of original pieces implies a seriousness the bar appreciates. Large pieces without much detail work best because of dim lighting conditions.

Artist handles installation. Nails OK. On the main level, there is a 30' by 8' wall and a 12' by 8' wall in the bar room, and a 15' by 12' brick wall in the dance area. There also is room for neon sculpture on a ledge three feet below ceiling level above the bathrooms. Club Dreamerz will consider sculpture for the beer garden. The mural in the beer garden changes each year, and artists may paint certain bar room walls.

Artist is responsible for insurance.

Artwork is purchased by contacting the artist directly. Club Dreamerz does not take a commission.

Openings are held on the second level. Club Dreamerz provides a keg and can make other arrangements on an individual basis.

Shows are promoted in weekly *Reader* ads. Club Dreamerz also advertises in *Illinois Entertainer* and on university radio stations. The bar does not supply a mailing list. Inside the club, the artist may place title cards next to each piece and leave additional information at the bar.

Club 950 Lucky Number
Dance Club

950 W. Wrightwood Avenue
Chicago, IL 60614
312/929-8955
Sun.-Fri., 9 p.m.-2 a.m.; Sat., 9 p.m.-3 a.m.

Noe Boudreau, Manager
1-Day Shows, 2-3 Times Yearly
Unrestricted

Not much to do at Club 950 but drink, dance and dance some more. The large open space and reasonable weekend cover of $3 attracts the stylish and not so stylish, but everyone there has a good time. The crowd ranges in age from 21-45, and is drawn from all over the city. The music is progressive, sometimes obscure, but always has a beat.

The look of the club changes every few months. Elaborate mobiles set seasonal themes matched by a musical emphasis. Occasional live acts are $3, and special events, like the art shows, are publicized in the *Reader*. The club celebrates its anniversary every August with a week of parties during the middle of that month.

Art Philosophy

Club 950 exhibits artwork to provide a refreshing change of pace. The shows bring in people who might not otherwise attend the club--they may like the place and come back. The shows also give something to the club's large artist clientele, most of whom are younger artists just getting started.

Shows are few and far between for two reasons. First, it is difficult to leave works hanging due to the crowds. Second, the club does not want the shows to be commonplace--interest is piqued when there are only two or three shows a year.

Like the general decor of Club 950, all art shows are themed. Themes are chosen by one of the DJs--one show featured women artists only. Club 950 stresses all creative forms. Video art is a strong focus.

Exhibiting

Make an appointment to present slides of work appropriate to the proposed theme for review. Exhibits are always group shows.

Artist handles installation. Nails OK. Gallery lights are installed around the perimeter of the club.

Artist is responsible for insurance.

Sales are cash and carry. Artist is present during the shows. Club 950 does not take a commission.

Shows are one-night dance parties open to the public and held on Sundays between 7:30 p.m. and 2 a.m. A $2 cover is charged.

Club 950 publicizes shows four weeks in advance in the *Reader* and on handbills mailed to the club's list and placed inside the club. During the shows, the artist can post prices next to each piece.

Diva Caffè
Coffee House

1802 N. Halsted Street
Chicago, IL 60614
312/266-9151
Sun.-Thurs., 7 a.m.-10 p.m.; Fri.-Sat., 7 a.m.-Midnight

Blake Dancer, Owner
Indefinite
Wall Hangings, Small Sculpture

A gently sloping ramp leads to a charming, well-groomed patio outside the Diva Caffè, quaint with wood, brick and potted flowers. The interior is spotless, white and pristine. Everything is meticulously positioned, down to the writing on two chalkboards that proclaim the coffee house's menu of sandwiches, pastries and coffees.

Strains of classical music and opera fill the room, and although there is no view of the Alps outside the storefront window, the atmosphere is very European. The clientele is a good mix of artists, musicians, professionals and neighborhood residents who come to read, converse and relax.

Art Philosophy

Diva Caffè exhibits artwork as part of its attempt to be authentically European.

The coffee house is seeking the artistic embodiment of the perfect Diva for display and promotional purposes.

Exhibiting

Make an appointment to present original pieces for review. Diva Caffè looks for works that blend with the European ambiance of the room. The coffee house normally hosts group shows of works in the same genre, but will consider single shows if the artist has strength.

Artist and the coffee house both handle installation. Nails OK. Two white walls are available, measuring about 35' by 12'.

Diva Caffè provides insurance for relatively inexpensive pieces. Artist is responsible for insuring very valuable work.

Artwork is purchased through Diva Caffè, which takes a 15-20 percent commission.

Openings are negotiable.

Artist is responsible for promotion. Inside the coffee house, the artist may place title cards next to each piece.

The Eccentric
Eclectic

159 W. Erie Street
Chicago, IL 60610
312/787-8390
Restaurant: Lunch: Mon.-Fri., 11:30 a.m.-2 p.m.; Dinner: Mon.-Thurs., 5:30 p.m.-10:30 p.m.; Fri.-Sat., 5 p.m.-11:30 p.m.; Sun., 5 p.m.-9 p.m.
Bar: Mon.-Thurs., 4:45 p.m.-Midnight; Fri.-Sat., 4:45 p.m.-1 a.m.; Sun., 5 p.m.-9 p.m.

Kevin Brown, Managing Partner
3 Months
Unrestricted

The Eccentric joins the ever-growing list of innovative ventures of the Lettuce Entertain You Corp. Oprah Winfrey lends her celebrity endorsement and a potato recipe to this restaurant that attracts an integrated crowd of fun-loving, sophisticated people, many of whom are Chicago's movers and shakers.

Large, open and lively, The Eccentric contains two dining rooms and three bar areas, each with a distinct character. The front is set up as a French café. It is long and narrow with a low wall. Thin columns divide it from the main Cocktail Room in the center of the space, the most social, mobile area (more a place to rest a drink than sit for a long time). Up and to the left is the Club Bar, a dark, woody area fashioned after an English smoking room, furnished with leather couches for lounging. To the right is the Gallery, an Italian-style section fashioned in Art Deco blacks and whites with leather-backed chairs and round tables. The back dining room is reminiscent of a Parisian salon, predominantly red, with black leather booths against the walls and circular tables scattered on the floor. The walls are covered with artwork from an impressive roster of local and international artists.

Expect to pay about $50 per couple for dinner.

Art Philosophy

The Eccentric exhibits artwork as an additional expression of creativity. As the restaurant's name implies, the works need to be eccentric, wild and offbeat. The hanging pieces are as artistic as the food prepared at The Eccentric.

Exhibiting

Make an appointment to present both slides and original pieces for review. Normally, The Eccentric hosts group shows.

The Eccentric handles installation. Nails OK.

Artist is responsible for insurance.

Artwork is purchased by contacting the artist directly. The Eccentric does not take a commission.

Openings are negotiable.

Artist is responsible for promotion. Inside the restaurant, no promotion is allowed--the pictures promote themselves. Artist's name and phone number can be obtained through the waitstaff or management.

Ennui Café
Coffee House

6981 N. Sheridan Road
Chicago, IL 60626
312/973-2233
Mon.-Thurs., 7:30 a.m.-10:30 p.m.; Fri., 7:30 a.m.-Midnight; Sat., 8 a.m.-Midnight; Sun., 9 a.m.-10:30 p.m.

Gail Eastman, Owner & Manager
2-3 Months
Wall Hangings

Despite its name, Ennui Café is far from boring. Set just below street level, the good-sized bright room is generally filled with students writing or reading, while others converse or just watch the street through the large windows. The black and white checkered floor is covered with loosely-placed green marble café tables and wooden chairs. Between the two entrances is a great private alcove, not too far removed from the action, with one table and a few chairs. The atmosphere is relaxed, with newspapers and other reading material resting on the window ledge for anyone interested.

In the summer, white tables are lined up outside, and items such as iced tea are added to the menu. The café serves coffees, teas, cappuccino, and light foods such as fruits, cheeses and pastries.

Art Philosophy

Ennui Café began exhibiting artwork on the initiative of one of its artist patrons. The pieces generated a positive reaction, and shows have continued ever since.

Ennui Café believes that black and white photographs are most consistent with the simple elegance of the interior.

Exhibiting

Make an appointment to present slides or original pieces for review. Group shows OK.

Artist handles installation. Two walls are available, one 10' by 10' and one 4' by 10'.

Artist is responsible for insurance.

Artwork is purchased by contacting the artist directly. Ennui Café does not take a commission.

Openings are negotiable.

Artist has access to the café's mailing list. Inside the café, the artist may post a price list and bio.

Esoteria
Dance Club

2247 N. Lincoln Avenue
Chicago, IL 60614
312/549-4110
Sun.-Fri., 3 p.m.-4 a.m.; Sat., 3 p.m.-5 a.m.

Jeff Taylor, Manager
Indefinite
Unrestricted

Esoteria is something between *Ben Hur* and *Beneath the Planet of the Apes*. Reliefs honoring Classical civilization decorate the walls of the bar room, which is dominated by a scene from the Sistine Chapel painted on an arched ceiling. The tables in the room are the sturdy bases of imposing columns. Thinner columns also rise from the floor, but halfway up twisted metal completes the form, giving a hint of what lies deeper inside.

Entering the dark recesses of the club, all sense of Antiquity disappears and one is in a mutant civilization, supported by twisted metal and pipes. Demon heads watch as the inhabitants go through their convulsions on the main dance floor and in a caged area off to the side. At the very back are more tables situated on a metal grate, the targets of random searchlights and laser bullets.

The clientele at Esoteria ranges from designers to traders. The Action Figures perform live on Monday, following Open Mike at 9 p.m. Wednesday is "Midnight at the Oasis" Night, with specials on sexually-oriented drinks. On Thursday, drinks for women are $1 from 8 p.m.-Midnight. All drinks are $1 during Sunday Beach Parties from 9 p.m.-Midnight. Cover is generally $4, except on Thursday, when it is $2. "Eso Food" includes New York soft pretzels, buffalo wings, fried calamari, fajitas, burgers and other sandwiches. All items are under $5.

Art Philosophy

Esoteria exhibits artwork to attract a clientele open to artistic expression.

Exhibiting

Make an appointment to present original pieces for review. Esoteria has dealt with a company called Happening Productions for one-day group shows.

Installation is handled by both Esoteria and the artist. Nails OK.

Artist is responsible for insurance.

Artwork is purchased by contacting the artist directly. Esoteria does not take a commission.

Esoteria will provide drink discounts for openings. Artist can bring in food or may use Esoteria's full-service catering facilities.

Promotion is primarily the artist's responsibility, but the club may assist. Artist must provide the bar with a mailing list indicating that the show will bring in new customers. Inside the club, the artist may post a price list, bio and title cards next to each piece.

Exit
Dance Club

1653 N. Wells Street
Chicago, IL 60610
312/440-0535
Mon.-Fri., 8 p.m.-4 a.m.; Sat., 6 p.m.-5 a.m.; Sun., 6 p.m.-4 a.m.

Joe, Manager
5 Weeks
Unrestricted

Welcome to the place just beyond Thunder Dome. Center stage at Exit, in black wardrobes, mohawked patrons bound, bounce, and sway in a sunken dance floor partially covered by a metal cage. Knives, axes, a chain saw and other weapons dangle from this wire canopy. Two raised cages off to either side of the dance floor are solo stages for anyone with the inclination to go it alone. Onlookers lean against the walls or rest on the ledge that borders the room.

The front room is brighter and holds a more subdued crowd. A narrow aisle divides the bar from a metal bench that runs along the wall. Two small televisions play *Batman* reruns to loud dance music. A small selection of bar snacks is available.

Nearly every night of the week is special at Exit. On Monday, $5 gets patrons all they can drink. Ladies drink free on Tuesday until Midnight. Wednesday is Bondage Night-- $3 lets patrons drink free from 8 p.m.-9 p.m., and ladies chained to the bar drink free all night. Thursday is Modern Music Night.

Art Philosophy

Exit exhibits artwork to keep its atmosphere interesting.

Murals by local artists decorate the interior and exterior walls of the club.

Exhibiting

Make an appointment to present slides or original pieces for review.

Artist handles installation. Work is suspended from the ceiling above the dance floor.

Artist is responsible for insurance.

Artwork is purchased by contacting the artist directly. Exit does not take a commission.

No formal openings.

Artist is responsible for promotion. Inside the club, the artist may post a price list.

F/X 1100
Dance Club

1100 N. State Street
Chicago, IL 60610
312/280-2282
Mon.-Fri., 4 p.m.-4 a.m.; Sat., 11 a.m.-5 a.m.; Sun., 11 a.m.-4 a.m.

Michael Povsher, PR Director
2 Weeks-1 Month
Unrestricted

With five levels and three bars, F/X 1100 offers a wide range of options. The space is sleek and mechanical, with modern, black and gray metal fixtures and a blue cast to the light. Every level is visible by at least one other area, giving the club an open feeling and providing ample vantage points for people watching. A mix of progressive and Top 40 music keeps the dance floor on the second level moving. From a large picture window, people on the street can view the dance floor and the large screen that occupies the wall behind it, running clips from movies and music videos. The rooftop garden, open during the summer, adds yet another dimension to the club.

F/X 1100's clientele is a mix of professionals and artists ranging in age from 25-35. The bar serves finger foods, ranging from french fries to escargot, sandwiches and breakfast after 1:00 a.m. Sunday is Future Star Talent Showcase, an Open Mike, and on Monday ladies drink free after 9 p.m. Cover is $5 on weekends.

Art Philosophy

F/X 1100 exhibits artwork to enhance its atmosphere and attract new groups of people to the bar.

After gallery openings, the parties often continue at F/X.

Exhibiting

F/X 1100 works with galleries and artists off the street. Make an appointment to present slides or original pieces for review. Videos also may be brought in for viewing.

Artist handles installation. There is one long wall available to the right of the entrance, and a wire grid on the ceiling above the bar where hooks can be fastened. F/X 1100 also has the technical resources to show video art. A 10' crushed pearl video screen, special effects video board, VHS and 3/4" formats are available.

Artist is responsible for insurance and must sign a waiver.

Artwork is purchased by contacting the artist directly. F/X 1100 does not take a commission.

Openings are scheduled on weeknights from 8 p.m.-10 p.m. or from 10 p.m.-Midnight. F/X 1100 will provide food and give each guest a free drink.

Artist has access to F/X's 5,000-person mailing list. The bar may print invitations. Inside the bar, the artist can display title cards, a price list and brochures.

Far Side, Inc.
Jazz

2957 W. Diversey Avenue
Chicago, IL 60647
312/772-5566
Mon.-Fri., 6 p.m.-2 a.m.; Sat., 6 p.m.-3 a.m.; Sun., 6 p.m.-Midnight

Judy Delphonse & Frank Mikulski, Co-Owners
1 Month
Wall Hangings

The Far Side is a neighborhood bar worth traveling to. It takes pride in showcasing new jazz and ethnic talent. The room is small and open to the street, thus creating an atmosphere brighter than that of most jazz clubs. Many plants in the windows attempt to make the storefront room more intimate.

The crowd at the Far Side is a mix of professionals under 35. Sunday through Wednesday, the bar is often reserved for parties won in frequent business-card drawings. Each guest gets free food, two free drinks and the chance at winning a Far Side T-shirt. For $10, patrons can join a beer club which offers drink and cover discounts, monthly meetings, and a free T-shirt when each of 50 different kinds of beer has been drunk. The club also offers a selection of board games for customer use.

Cover on the seven weekly nights of entertainment ranges from $2-5 after 9 p.m.

Art Philosophy

The Far Side's goal is to provide a showcase for fresh new talent in music and visual art. The club is a place for the musician and the artist to perfect their respective crafts. The Far Side recognizes the problems of exposure artists face and believes its neighborhood is ripe with potential art buyers. Art also benefits the club by adding to its atmosphere.

Exhibiting

The Far Side prefers to review original pieces in order to get a feel for them in the room.

The Far Side supervises installation and lighting. There is a large display wall behind the stage, and space for smaller pieces over the windows that surround the bar. The Far Side will remove beer signs in order to accommodate the artist's work.

Artist is responsible for insurance, but the bar does have a security system.

Artwork is purchased by contacting the artist directly. The Far Side does not take a commission.

Openings are arranged individually, depending on the number of people expected. Wine discounts are provided.

The Far Side generates flyers and publicizes exhibits in a monthly calendar. 1,000 flyers are distributed to the 250+ beer club members and to neighborhood residents, and an additional 250 are given to the artist. Inside the bar, promotional materials may be displayed at the artist's discretion.

Gentry and the Café
American/Piano Lounge

712 N. Rush Street
Chicago, IL 60611
312/664-1033
Café: Sun.-Sat., 5 p.m.-Midnight
Bar: Sun.-Fri., 4 p.m.-2 a.m.; Sat., 4 p.m.-3 a.m.

Dave Edwards, Owner & Manager
2-3 Months
Wall Hangings

Set in a beautiful, old three-story building, Gentry and the Café is a comfortable, friendly club in which to unwind. The clientele consists mostly of gay businessmen who stop in for a drink after work. Later in the evening, stage lights focus attention on live piano music, offered seven nights a week without charge.

Upstairs, the dining room has two levels, each with its own fireplace. Fresh flowers adorn every table. The café serves a traditional menu, including steaks, pork and chicken dishes. Expect to pay about $30 per couple for dinner.

Art Philosophy

Gentry and the Café exhibits artwork to enhance its atmosphere. The clientele enjoys seeing new, original work.

Exhibiting

Make an appointment to present work for review. Slides OK. Gentry and the Café will consider group shows.

Artist handles installation. Nails OK. There are two 10' by 12' walls, one 12' by 12' wall, one 8' by 12' wall, and four 3' by 12' walls in the restaurant and foyer.

Artist is responsible for insurance and must sign a waiver.

Artwork is purchased by contacting the artist directly. Gentry and the Café does not take a commission.

Openings are negotiable.

Artist has access to Gentry's 1,200-name mailing list. Gentry and the Café will tag information about exhibits in gay newspapers if the artist wishes. Inside the club, the artist may post a price list or place title cards next to each piece.

Grant's Tavern & Grill
Tavern

2138 N. Halsted Street
Chicago, IL 60614
312/348-3665
Sun.-Fri., 11 a.m.-2 a.m.; Sat., 11 a.m.-3 a.m.

Lin Liston, Manager
1 Month-6 Weeks
Wall Hangings

Grant's Tavern & Grill is an unpretentious American bar. The clientele skews yuppie, and comes to hang out and have a good time with friends. A gathering place for social activity, Grant's offers incentives such as raffling off parties and sponsoring athletic teams.

The food at Grant's is fresh, and the sandwiches, soups and salads come in large portions at reasonable prices. Expect to pay between $15-20 per couple for dinner and drinks.

Art Philosophy

Artwork provides an additional sensory stimulation that combines with the food, the music and the people to make going out more of an event. If you're not stimulated, you might as well drink at home. Changing the art keeps Grant's dynamic.

Grant's Tavern & Grill sees art as a way to expose people to different ideas. There is interaction about the art, and regular patrons often inquire about future shows.

Exhibiting

Make an appointment to present slides or original pieces for review. Group shows OK.

Artist handles installation. Nails OK. There is wall space for about seven pieces per show, measuring as large as 5' by 4'.

Artist is responsible for insurance.

Artwork is purchased by contacting the artist directly. Grant's Tavern & Grill does not take a commission.

Openings are negotiable.

Grant's Tavern & Grill prints cards to promote exhibits and sends them to people on the bar's mailing list. Additional cards are given to the artist. Inside the bar, a price list and bio are placed near the entrance, and more price lists and business cards can be left at the bar.

Guthries Tavern
Tavern

1300 W. Addison Street
Chicago, IL 60613
312/477-2900
Sun.-Fri., 4 p.m.-2 a.m.; Sat., 4 p.m.-3 a.m. (Open earlier for Cub games)

Steve Leith, Owner
1-2 Months
Unrestricted

Guthries Tavern is a friendly neighborhood bar that calls to mind a New England coastal town. It has a rustic feel and is decorated with nautical fixtures and prints. A white picket fence surrounds a flower-filled patio. The over-all atmosphere is one of comfort and relaxation.

Art Philosophy

Guthries Tavern exhibits artwork because it provides neighborhood artists with valuable exposure. Art is interesting for the bar owner and the patrons.

Exhibiting

Reviews are informal. Neither slides nor original pieces are necessary, just a serious, follow-through attitude. As long as work is in good taste, it can be exhibited.

Artist handles installation. A 20' by 10' wall in the middle room is reserved for hanging pieces. Nails OK. Sculpture may be installed in the garden.

Artist is responsible for insurance.

Artwork is purchased by contacting the artist directly. Guthries Tavern does not take a commission.

Openings are negotiable.

Artist is responsible for promotion. Guthries Tavern does not have a mailing list. Inside the bar, promotional materials may be displayed at the artist's discretion.

Heartland Cafe, General Store & Buffalo Bar
Café/Tavern

7000 N. Glenwood Avenue
Chicago, IL 60626
312/465-8005
Mon.-Fri., 9 a.m.-2 a.m.; Sat., 9 a.m.-3 a.m.; Sun., 9 a.m.-2 a.m.

Michael James, Co-Director, General Store & Buffalo Bar
2 Months
Unrestricted

Large and airy, the Heartland is a comfortable spot conducive to relaxed conversation, quiet reading or hanging out. An inviting patio dominates the front of the café, and becomes the most animated area of the restaurant during the warm months.

Inside, the space is divided into three distinct sections. At the entrance is the General Store, where clothing, books, arts and crafts, and healthy foods are sold. Deeper into the space is the Buffalo Bar--small, dark and rustic. Farther back is the main dining room, a big, bright, divided space with mis-matched wooden furniture.

The Heartland Cafe, General Store & Buffalo Bar offers a full menu, including vegetarian dishes, chicken and fish. Buffalo meat sometimes is available in the Buffalo Bar. Live music is performed on Friday through Sunday. Cover is $3 before 11 p.m.

Art Philosophy

The Heartland Cafe, General Store & Buffalo Bar exhibits artwork in support of the local artistic community.

Exhibiting

Make an appointment to present slides or original works for review or schedule a studio visitation.

Artist handles installation on two 30' walls. Nails OK.

The Heartland Cafe, General Store & Buffalo Bar provides insurance for exhibited artwork.

Artwork is purchased through the Heartland, which takes a 20-40 percent commission.

Openings are scheduled between 4 p.m. and 6 p.m. on weekdays. Half of the restaurant is reserved for the reception and arrangements can be made to serve wine and appetizers.

Artist has access to the Heartland's mailing list for promotion. The Heartland Cafe, General Store & Buffalo Bar also publishes a listing about each exhibit in its newsletter, the *Heartland Journal*. Inside the café, the artist can post a price list and bio.

Izimbra
Tavern

2724 N. Lincoln Avenue
Chicago, IL 60614
312/935-1214
Sun.-Fri., Noon-2 a.m.; Sat., Noon-3 a.m.

John & Jim Burns, Co-Owners
1 Month
Unrestricted

Izimbra, named after the nonsense rhythmic background of a Dada tone poem, creates the atmosphere of a renovated garage. The large glass door is rolled up in the summer for outdoor seating. Inside, a long bar runs the stretch of wall to the right of the entrance, past a group of tables scattered by the garage door. The bar reaches a white back wall, spotted like a dalmation. Videos, played on a screen on top of this wall, accompany music ranging from Buddy Holly to the Sex Pistols.

Izimbra attracts a mix of professionals, artists and rock 'n' rollers aged 25-45. The bar offers games like foosball and electronic bowling, and summer billiards under the stars in the beer garden. Izimbra serves traditional bar snacks, sandwiches and chili. On an impromptu basis, usually in the winter, the bar schedules month-long runs of comedy shows or weekly poetry readings. Cover is $3-5 for these special events.

Art Philosophy

In the Dada tradition, Izimbra seeks to be an innovative and ever-changing place. The bar exhibits new artwork to provide its patrons with interesting things to look at and interact with.

Izimbra is interested in student work if it shows potential.

Exhibiting

Make an appointment to present slides or original pieces for review. In special cases, Izimbra will make studio visits.

Artist handles installation. Two walls measuring 32' by 10' and 14' by 10' are available. Track lighting is in place above the long wall. Additionally, a cinder block wall leading to the beer garden is offered as mural space.

Izimbra provides insurance covering the price of exhibited artwork.

Openings begin at 9 p.m. on the first Friday or Saturday of the month. Terms are negotiable.

Izimbra will promote exhibits in normal mailings, and will generate invitations from an artist sketch. Inside the bar, the artist may post a price list, bio and title cards next to each piece.

Java Jive
Coffee House

909 W. School Street
Chicago, IL 60657
312/549-3500
Mon.-Thurs., 7:30 a.m.-Midnight; Fri., 7:30 a.m.-After Midnight;
Sat., 8 p.m.-After Midnight; Sun., 10 a.m.-11 p.m.

Cheryl Blumenthal, Proprietor
1 Month
Unrestricted

Java Jive is a happy, bright and bustling coffee house that seems always to be crowded and loud with animated conversation. It's just plain fun to be part of the mixed group of artists and professionals surrounded by wild and colorful art. Art is everywhere you look at Java Jive. It consumes the entire space, but does not suffocate the customers. It fits in naturally with and adds to the lively atmosphere of the room.

Java Jive serves up a wide range of light, natural foods including soups, sandwiches, salads, cheeses and fruits in addition to coffee, cider, tea and cappuccino. Meghan Wade reads tarot cards for $10 on Thursday from 8:30 p.m.-Midnight and on Sunday from 6:30 p.m.-11 p.m. On occasion, entertainment from street performers is offered. Cover is at the discretion of the customer.

Art Philosophy

Java Jive is set up as a networking environment for artists and collectors. The café believes it is important to give exposure to artists who are just starting out, and to give collectors the chance to purchase unique and affordable local work. Gallery owners have given shows to artists they "discovered" at Java Jive.

Exhibiting

Make an appointment to present slides and a representative original piece for review. Java Jive will make studio visits to see large works.

Artist handles installation. Wall pieces are hung from picture rails. There are two 12' by 10' walls with track lighting and space for pieces in the bathroom. Small sculptural pieces may be placed on the piano.

Java Jive provides insurance for exhibited artwork.

Artwork is purchased by contacting the artist directly. The coffee house will take a deposit to hold a piece for a patron. Java Jive does not take a commission.

If the artist chooses to have an opening, it is scheduled on a Monday or Tuesday night from 7 p.m.-9 p.m.

Artist is responsible for promotion. Java Jive will give the artist access to its mailing list. Inside the coffee house, the artist may number pieces and place a price list on the piano.

Jean Claude
French

2442 N. Clark Street
Chicago, IL 60614
312/525-1800
Mon.-Fri., 4 p.m.-1 a.m.; Sat.-Sun., 11 a.m.-2 a.m.

Carole Gutierrez
Indefinite
Wall Hangings

Jean Claude offers a sense of the simple ease and elegance of French Provincial living. Softly faded wallpaper, cozy wooden furnishings, brick fireplaces, low lighting and quiet classical music transport the patron into a more tranquil era.

There are four dining rooms at Jean Claude, each with its own atmosphere. The two front rooms are small and intimate. The back rooms are slightly larger and more social, as a result of a bar that divides the two spaces. Up a narrow stairway, a private dining room hosts parties of up to 60 people. In the summer, outdoor dining is provided on a raised deck supported by colorfully muraled walls.

Jean Claude attracts a mixed crowd of students and professionals. Dress ranges from casual to semi-formal. Expect to pay about $40 per couple for dinner. Brunch is served on Saturday and Sunday.

Art Philosophy

Jean Claude exhibits artwork as enrichment for the clientele and for the benefit of the artist.

Exhibiting

Make an appointment to present slides and a representative original piece for review. Jean Claude seeks more realistic works, but will look at abstract pieces if they are not too bizarre.

Artist handles installation. Nails OK. There is ample wall space on both levels. Pieces are typically 2-1/2' by 3'.

Artist is responsible for insurance.

Artwork is purchased by contacting the artist directly. Jean Claude does not take a commission.

Openings are negotiable.

Artist has access to the restaurant's mailing list. Inside the restaurant, the artist may post a bio, price list and title cards next to each piece.

Jerome's
American

2450 N. Clark Street
Chicago, IL 60614
312/327-2207
Sun., 10 a.m.-11 p.m.; Mon., 5 p.m.-11 p.m.; Tue.-Thurs., 11:30 a.m.-11 p.m.; Fri., 11:30 a.m.-Midnight; Sat., 9 a.m.-Midnight (Café hours extended in summer)

Jerome Kliejunas, Owner & Manager
6 Months
Wall Hangings

Jerome's is as informal as its outdoor café, as social as its bar, and as elegant as its dining room. The restaurant is many things to many people, and attracts a mix of neighborhood residents, artists and professionals.

The entrance opens into a narrow room containing the bar. The space is dimly lit and filled with activity. The bar itself is a rich wood, topped by rows of wine glasses and lined by chairs covered in a soft floral print. Above the bar is a mural, painted wild and bright, and to the left is a cluster of small, intimate tables.

An arched doorway leads to the main dining area. There is a seemingly endless expanse of ceiling lights, reflected in a large mirror on the back wall. The room is simple yet elegant. The walls are painted in soft pastels, and a mahogany molding runs the length of the room. Jerome's regular menu includes a variety of entrees, all under $10. Daily specials feature fresh fish, meat and pasta. Expect to pay about $30 per couple for dinner.

Art Philosophy

Jerome's exhibits artwork in support of the aspiring artists employed by the restaurant--only employees are allowed to have shows.

Exhibiting

Apply for a job at Jerome's. Once an employee, submit slides or original pieces for review, for shows scheduled twice a year. Group shows are selected from the staff's work.

Artist and management handle installation. Nails OK.

Artist is responsible for insurance.

Artwork is purchased by contacting the artist directly. Interested patrons leave their names and numbers at the bar if the artist is not present. Artist will contact the prospective buyers. Pieces may not be removed from the walls until a replacement is ready.

Openings are catered by Jerome's, and include finger foods, house wine, beer on tap and coffee.

Jerome's promotes the exhibits, appropriately named "Behind the Apron." Notices are placed on each table in the restaurant and invitations to openings are mailed to a combined list. Openings also are listed in the *Reader*'s calendar section. Inside the restaurant, the artist may place small numbers next to each piece and leave a price list and bio at the bar.

The Lizard Lounge
Dance Club

1824 W. Augusta Boulevard
Chicago, IL 60622
312/489-0379
Wed.-Fri., 9 p.m.-2 a.m.; Sat., 9 p.m.-3 a.m.

Scot & Sharon, Managers
6 Weeks-2 Months
Unrestricted

Even though The Lizard Lounge is off the beaten path, it often fills to capacity. Young artists find their way to this fun and spirited spot to dance and socialize. The bar room is large and noisy, and murals of partying reptiles surround the dance floor.

The Lizard Lounge serves a unique selection of snacks, including Ho-Hos, potato chips and cheese popcorn. The bar offers half-price drinks on Wednesday and Thursday until Midnight. Cover is $2 on Friday and Saturday.

Art Philosophy

The Lizard Lounge exhibits artwork as a source of public feedback for new artists. Patrons appreciate the exhibits and the changes in club atmosphere they create.

The Lizard Lounge seeks art that is unusual and daring.

Exhibiting

Make an appointment to present slides or original pieces for review. Group shows OK.

Artist handles installation on the long wall across from the bar. Nails OK. Sculpture also may be placed in the front room.

Artist is responsible for insurance and must sign a waiver.

Works are purchased by contacting the artist directly. The Lizard Lounge does not take a commission.

Informal openings are usually scheduled early on Friday nights. The Lizard Lounge provides drink discounts for guests.

Promotion is the joint responsibility of the artist and the bar. The Lizard Lounge does not have a mailing list, but the club will promote exhibits in regular *Reader* ads. Inside the bar, promotion is low-key. Artist may place title cards next to each piece and leave a phone number at the bar.

The Local Option
Tavern

1102 W. Webster Avenue
Chicago, IL 60614
312/348-2008 or 312/525-8528
Sun.-Fri., 5 p.m.-2 a.m.; Sat., 5 p.m.-3 a.m.

Hugh Haller, Owner
6 Weeks-2 Months
Unrestricted

The Local Option's name comes from a political fight that took place in the neighborhood before the bar opened. A group of citizens, exercising its local option to vote the precinct dry when it heard a new bar was being built, collected enough signatures to prevent the establishment from opening. An intense outreach campaign by the bar changed enough minds so that it could open as planned.

The Local Option deliberately provides a generic atmosphere in order to defy classification. The bar strives to remain fresh and interesting, never to be shoved into a rigid category. The mood of the bar changes with the musical tastes of the bartenders. The space is long, crooked and narrow. Past the bar is a pool table, and beyond a narrow corridor is a small sitting room. The diverse crowd ranges between the ages of 23-35. Bar snacks, like pizza and Sliders, are served.

Art Philosophy

The Local Option exhibits artwork as another way of defying classification. Each show creates a different mood by attracting new types of people and stimulating diverse conversation. The Local Option's reputation as an alternative space for art has been growing, and the quality of the shows has steadily increased. The shows are being taken seriously and response has been favorable.

Bizarre, humorous abstract pieces work best at The Local Option. The bar will not accept very commercial pieces, like portraits of famous characters or country scenes, and will probably turn away nudes or heavy political statements. Photographs do not normally work unless they are large.

Exhibiting

Contact The Local Option by phone or in writing. Persistence is important. The bar prefers to see original pieces for review, or at least one that is representative of the proposed show. The bar has worked with galleries and is open to group shows, as long as one artist takes the lead in getting things together.

The Local Option handles installation. Nails OK. The bar demands that the artist have enough work to fill the entire space--the average number of pieces is 12, several of which must measure at least 3' by 6'.

Artist is responsible for insurance.

Artwork is purchased by contacting the artist directly. The Local Option does not take a commission. So far, exhibiting artists have sold about half their work.

Openings are held two weeks after each show begins. The bar will provide drink discounts and will allow the artist to bring in food.

Artist is responsible for promotion. Inside the bar, the artist can post a bio and price list, leave information at the bar, and place title cards next to each piece.

Lounge Ax
Alternative Rock

2438 N. Lincoln Avenue
Chicago, IL 60614
312/525-6620
Daily, 4 p.m.-2 a.m.

Julia Adams & Jennifer Fischer, Co-Owners
3-4 Months
Unrestricted

Lounge Ax is a small, spirited club with loud music and little light. A big video screen provides much of the room's illumination, and divides the front bar area from a larger performance space in the back.

The clientele of young artists can lounge in comfortable booths across from the bar and listen or dance to live musical acts with an experimental edge. Cover is $2-5. Lounge Ax does not serve food, but patrons may bring their own or even order in.

Art Philosophy

Lounge Ax exudes enthusiasm for the local art scene. Its energetic atmosphere is a result of specific tie-ins it establishes with current events in the artistic community. The club has sponsored book openings, featured upcoming musicians, and made its building front a canvas for Chicago artists.

Exhibiting

Make an appointment to present slides or original pieces for review. Group shows OK.

Artist handles installation. Nails OK. There is an 18' by 12' wall available across the bar with decent light. Along this wall and 3' beneath the ceiling is a shelf for small objects.

Artist is responsible for insurance.

Artwork is purchased by contacting the artist directly. While Lounge Ax does not take a commission, the bar will accept a piece out of each show as thanks or negotiate a reduced rate.

Lounge Ax will provide drink discounts at openings.

Artist has access to the bar's mailing list for promotion. Inside the bar, the artist may post a price list, bio, and title cards next to each piece.

Maxtavern
Tavern

2856 N. Racine Avenue
Chicago, IL 60657
312/348-5055
Sun.-Fri., 1:30 p.m.-2 a.m.; Sat., 1:30 p.m.-3 a.m.

Anyone on Staff
2 Weeks +
Unrestricted

Like most bars, Maxtavern has framed its "first dollar," but to go along with its theme of world peace, the first lira, pound, peso and franc also have been framed. Globes rest on the bar and hang from the ceiling for the same reason.

Maxtavern lies in a tiny unmarked building on a quiet residential street. The pistachio-green room is conversational, with an eclectic clientele of artists, designers and professionals. There are no videos for distraction, just great background music spun by the bartenders from an extensive collection. The room fills quickly, but one can arrive early and save one of the few small tables in the back, near a photo booth, pinball machine and Skill Crane.

Art Philosophy

Maxtavern exhibits artwork when it is something of interest to the community. Art can be educational and fun.

Maxtavern has hosted parties and exhibits for The Peace Museum and other nonprofit arts organizations.

Exhibiting

Stop in, see the place, and talk to one of the bartenders. Maxtavern is very informal and flexible if the artist is serious. Group shows OK.

Installation is handled by both the artist and bar. There are nails high on the tin walls from which fish wire is hung. Scattered space is available on three walls, and objects may be placed on top of the photo booth.

Artist is responsible for insurance.

Artwork is purchased by contacting the artist directly. Maxtavern does not take a commission.

Openings are negotiable.

Maxtavern may help with promotion by generating flyers around the exhibit. Inside the bar, the artist can post a bio and price list.

Medici Gallery and Coffee House
Pizzeria

1450 E. 57th Street
Chicago, IL 60637
312/667-7394
Mon.-Thurs., 11:30 a.m.-12:30 a.m.; Fri., 11:30 a.m.-1:30 a.m.; Sat., 9 a.m.-1:30 a.m.; Sun., 9 a.m-12:30 a.m.

Manager
Indefinite
Wall Hangings

The Medici Gallery and Coffee House calls to mind a Medieval banquet hall. On the way inside the dining room, one passes a religious statue before being greeted by a giant moose head mounted on the wall. The room itself is dark and smoky, with dim light radiating from cone-shaped, wrought-iron fixtures that dangle from the ceiling. The furniture is big and wooden, and the air is filled with music, conversation, and the smell of good food. As a laid-back place to get a quick, inexpensive meal--usually pizza or a burger--Medici caters to a largely student clientele.

Watch for Medici Gallery and Coffee House's new location.

Art Philosophy

Art fits the atmosphere and environs of Medici. Hyde Park, in which the restaurant is located, boasts the city's oldest annual art fair and a student population that likes to be involved with the art scene.

Exhibiting

Make an appointment to present slides or original pieces for review.

Artist handles installation. Nails OK. There is a 15' wall on the left side of the dining room that can accommodate large pieces. Smaller work can be hung between the booths on the right side of the room.

Artist is responsible for insurance.

Artwork is purchased by contacting the artist directly. Medici Gallery and Coffee House does not take a commission.

Openings are negotiable.

Artist is responsible for promoting exhibits. Inside the restaurant, the artist may discreetly post a price list and bio.

Medusa's
Dance Club

3257 N. Sheffield Avenue
Chicago, IL 60657
312/935-3635
Wed., 10 p.m.-2 a.m.; Fri., 9 p.m.-2 a.m.; Sat., 7 p.m.-10 p.m.--All Ages,
11 p.m.-3 a.m.--Ages 17+

Tom Hemingway
2 Weeks-1 Month
Unrestricted

Medusa's is a three-story funhouse filled with passageways and themed rooms wild enough to satisfy the most adventurous patrons. On the first level, the mouth of a giant clown is the entrance into the main dance floor. The room is dark, but streamers and brightly painted pillars that function as dance stages add color. This carnival is the largest room in the house.

The remaining two floors are broken up into several smaller spaces. Walking through, one encounters plaster Buddhas and female mannequin torsos fitted with "biological clocks." The second floor contains a live rock room that offers Heavy Metal on Friday and Saturday, and a balcony giving a full view of the main dance floor. The Pagoda Lounge, a video dance space, occupies the third floor near a square gallery with couches and enclosed glass cases in which artwork is displayed.

Medusa's caters to an upscale, modern, highly experimental group of 17 to 25 year olds. No alcohol is served here, but juice bar or not, one needs an I.D. to get inside. Cover is $5 on Wednesday, $3 with a college I.D., $5 on Friday and $7 on Saturday.

Art Philosophy

Medusa's exhibits artwork to support the arts and the local artistic community. The club has launched the careers of several young artists.

Exhibiting

Make an appointment to present slides or original pieces for review. Group shows OK.

Artist handles installation, usually on the first of the month. Work is displayed inside glass cases that measure about 4' by 8'.

Artist is responsible for insurance. Display cases are locked.

Artwork is purchased by contacting the artist directly or through Medusa's, which does not take a commission.

Opening receptions are normally held the first Friday of the month before the club opens. Drink discounts are negotiable.

Artist uses his or her own mailing list for promotion, but Medusa's has facilities to generate flyers. Inside the club, the artist may post a bio, price list and title cards next to each piece.

No Exit Café-Gallery
Jazz, Folk/Coffee House

6970 N. Glenwood Avenue
Chicago, IL 60626
312/743-3355
Mon.-Thurs., 4 p.m.-Midnight; Fri., 4 p.m.-1 a.m.; Sat., Noon-1 a.m.;
Sun., Noon-Midnight

Bryan & Sue Kozin
6-7 Weeks
Wall Hangings

No Exit Café-Gallery is the oldest folk coffee house in the nation. Brown burlap stretched along the walls, two large ceiling fans hanging lazily from a white textured ceiling, and raw wooden furniture create an informal atmosphere where people come to relax. The low hum of conversation provides a background for those who just want to read. One may bring in reading material or choose from a selection of books jammed on shelves in a little alcove in the rear of the room. Board games also are available for a rental fee of 50¢ per hour. No Exit Café-Gallery offers a light menu of soups, salads, sandwiches, coffee, espresso and cappuccino.

Music, however, is the main focus at No Exit. A stage dominates the room, which fills with folk, jazz and light opera every day but Tuesday. Cover is as advertised Sunday through Wednesday--often a hat will be passed around. On Thursday, cover is $1.50-2.50, and $3-6 on Friday and Saturday.

Art Philosophy

No Exit Café-Gallery exhibits artwork to support the local artistic community and to keep its atmosphere fresh and alive.

Exhibiting

Make an appointment to present slides representative of the proposed show for review.

Artist handles installation. There are two walls that take nails and another wall with molding for gallery hooks.

Artist is responsible for insurance.

Artwork is purchased by contacting the artist directly. No Exit Café-Gallery does not take a commission.

Openings are scheduled on Sundays from 1 p.m.-4 p.m., catching the beginning of a jazz set by Bob Dogen that starts at 3:30 p.m.

Promotion is the artist's responsibility. One of No Exit's regulars generally makes a calligraphy window sign for the artist.

Northside Cafe
Tavern

939 W. Webster Avenue
Chicago, IL 60614
312/477-6662
Mon.-Fri., 4 p.m.-2 a.m.; Sat.-Sun., 11 a.m.-2 a.m.

Cyril Landise, Owner
1 Month
Unrestricted

Northside Cafe is the only widely acknowledged art bar in the city. It is a mecca for local creatives to discuss the art world and the works it produces.

The bar is small, intimate and narrow, with a row of cabaret tables across from a straight, stool-lined bar. Muraled walls suggest dynamism and movement, and provide a striking background for the artwork displayed. Outside, the urban garden under the El tracks provides a stimulating atmosphere for summer drinking and dining.

The mood inside the Northside changes with each bartender's taste in music, videos and friends. It can be relaxed or boisterous. Monday is Open Mike, and on Tuesday there are live performances ranging from traditional Irish music to acoustic rock. There is never a cover.

Pizza slices from O'Famé are available as a snack or dinner. Weekend brunch is served. Egg dishes come with a fruit and bread plate and homemade hash browns for under $6.

Watch for the Northside Cafe's new location.

Art Philosophy

Northside Cafe exhibits artwork in support of all art, but particularly local art, and the struggle to make it better. The purpose is to create a meaningful discourse about the production of art, to cause people to appreciate the process of making art. Interaction among customers and employees about the exhibits is a beneficial intellectual exercise.

A repairman made the whole thing worthwhile when, dirty from working on the bar's refrigerator, he exclaimed, "This shit really moves me."

Exhibiting

Make an appointment to present slides and/or original pieces for review. Group shows are OK as long as there is a reason for the pieces to be together. All shows should be thematic in some way. The bar discourages photographs.

Installation is the artist's responsibility, and is done on the day the show opens. Lighting is set up for about eight 20" by 20" pieces. Nails are already in place on the two available hanging walls, but more can be added. For small sculptural works, shelves may be installed. Larger sculpture is reserved for the urban garden. Video work may be shown on two medium-sized monitors.

Artist is responsible for insurance.

Artwork is purchased by contacting the artist directly. Northside Café does not take a commission.

Openings are informal gatherings by artist invitation with no drink discounts. The artist is encouraged to use the stage for a performance around the exhibit during the opening.

Northside Café will assist in developing promotional material at the artist's request, but the artist is responsible for distribution. Inside the bar, the artist must hang a framed bio and price list.

Not Just Pasta
Diner

2965 N. Lincoln Avenue
Chicago, IL 60657
312/348-2842
Mon., 5 p.m.-Midnight; Tue.-Fri., 11 a.m.-Midnight; Sat.-Sun., 8 a.m.-Midnight

Edward Krajewski, Chef & Owner
1-3 Months
Unrestricted

Informal and reasonably priced, Not Just Pasta is a 1950s-style diner filled with polished chrome. The room is plain and cozy, with simple tables and chairs arranged on a wooden floor. The restaurant attracts an upscale, fun-loving clientele.

Pasta is the specialty, but a wide selection of sandwiches, salads and meat dishes rounds out the menu. Wine or beer may be brought in for a $2 service fee. For dinner, expect to pay about $20 per couple. Reservations are accepted for parties of six or more.

Art Philosophy

Visual art complements the culinary art of Not Just Pasta. The restaurant provides a showcase for people trying to express themselves. Not Just Pasta and its clientele both benefit from the constant change of rotating exhibits.

Not Just Pasta will reject artwork that is extremely grotesque.

Exhibiting

Send a letter of interest describing work and artistic goals. Group shows OK.

Artist handles installation. Nails OK. Scattered wall space can hold pieces measuring 6' by 8' and smaller. Artist must come in on a regular basis to clean and maintain the artwork.

Artist is responsible for insurance.

Artwork is purchased by contacting the artist directly. Pieces in the $50-500 range sell best. Not Just Pasta does not take a commission.

Not Just Pasta will provide food at openings; artist may bring wine.

Not Just Pasta will give the artist access to 4,000 names and write a press release about the exhibit. Inside the restaurant, the artist may post information about the show and leave a stack of price lists on a small ledge near the entrance.

Outtakes
NightClub

16 W. Ontario Street
Chicago, IL 60610
312/951-7979
Sun.-Fri., 4 p.m.-2 a.m.; Sat., 4 p.m.-3 a.m.

Ira Sapir, Owner & Tim, Promotion
1 Month
Photographs

As you open the gate to Outtakes, a large mural leads you down a staircase into a dark, blue room. You have now entered an underwater world. The place is predominantly lit with blue tank light radiating from a stool-lined bar. The countertop is a fish tank, filled with an exotic mix of tropical fish. The motif is carried into a brighter, more intimate back room with shell-like fixtures and booths for privacy grouped around a central tank.

The crowd at Outtakes is a mix of design professionals, businesspeople, artists and tourists. A side room off the main bar offers dancing nightly to progressive music. Cover is $3. Every Sunday is Reggae Night. Outside, Reggae and Brazilian music are played in the Concrete Jungle, a beer garden surrounded by tropical trees made of steel and illuminated by colored lights. For the hungry, Outtakes offers a selection of snacks, including pizza bread, hot dogs and chicken wings.

Art Philosophy

Outtakes is serious about photography. Over the bar is an extensive collection of vintage cameras, and the walls are always available for unique and interesting photographic works. The name Outtakes describes the bar's philosophy of showing works that might not otherwise be shown, images that tend toward the outrageous, the offbeat, and the controversial. The bar recognizes the emotional power that good photography can convey.

At the time of Outtakes' opening in 1987, it was the only gallery showing strictly photography. By supporting the local photographic community, Outtakes keeps its atmosphere fresh with innovative work.

Exhibiting

Make an appointment to present a portfolio for review and discuss your work. Outtakes looks for noncommercial, wild, controversial pieces. Group shows OK.

Outtakes handles installation, but the artist may be present. Nails OK. The artist's work must at least be matted; Outtakes will provide glass if necessary. There are three walls available, two by the main bar and one in the hallway leading to the back room. They measure about 20' by 10', 6' by 10', and 12' by 10'. Track lighting is installed to spot each piece.

Artist is responsible for insurance.

Artwork is purchased through Outtakes, which takes a 40 percent commission. The bar will often buy a piece or two. Artist may replace pieces as they are sold or leave them up for the show's duration.

Openings are held the first Tuesday of every month from 7 p.m.-9 p.m., with a beer and wine reception.

Outtakes prints color invitations and mails them to a 1,200-name mailing list. Inside the club, the artist may post a price list near the first piece in the exhibit and place title cards next to each piece.

Pastafina
Italian

921 W. Belmont Avenue
Chicago, IL 60657
312/528-4499
Mon.-Thurs., 11 a.m.-9 p.m.; Fri.-Sat., 11 a.m.-10 p.m.; Sun., 3 p.m.-8 p.m.

Susan Santacaterina, Owner
3 Months
Wall Hangings

This small, bright and clean restaurant comes complete with a black and white checkered floor, white café tables, and raw wood chairs. Lots of regular customers give Pastafina a neighborhood feel. It is a place to sit and hang out.

In the back, a white tile counter handsomely displays fresh pasta, salads and antipasti to take out or eat in. Pastafina cuts its pasta in a variety of styles, served with a choice of five sauces. Pasta dinners are about $6.

Art Philosophy

Pastafina lends itself to showing art because of its small size and intimate, European atmosphere.

The restaurant prefers photographs or abstract works with lots of color.

Exhibiting

Make an appointment to present slides or original pieces for review.

Artist handles installation. Small nails are OK, as the walls do not support much weight. A 15' by 4' wall is available across from a semi-permanent group of photographs, and there is room for two 4' by 4' pieces by the counter.

Artist is responsible for insurance.

Artwork is purchased by contacting the artist directly. Pastafina does not take a commission.

No formal openings.

Pastafina will promote exhibits in its bi-monthly newsletter, displayed in-store and mailed to 150 patrons. No posted prices are allowed inside, but the artist may display a bio with an address and phone number.

Phyllis' Musical Inn
Tavern

1800 W. Division Street
Chicago, IL 60622
312/486-9862
Daily, 1 p.m.-2 a.m.

Clem Jaskot, Manager
Indefinite
Unrestricted

Phyllis Jaskot started Phyllis' Musical Inn in 1953 as a Polish-American bar with lots of polka music and dancing. Today, while the original bar, piano and wallpaper still exist, the music is contemporary and the crowd is mixed. Other additions include bright, kitschy murals done by local artists that decorate the stage and entranceway, and a public radio banner that hangs behind the stage.

Four nights a week, the small recessed stage livens up with jazz, blues and rock artists. Patrons can dance on a small floor in front of the stage, sit and drink farther away by the bar, just listen to the music in a small section of row seats salvaged from a neighborhood church, or get away from it all in the summer in the backyard beer garden. Expect a $2-3 cover on weekends. Thursday night is DJ Night.

Art Philosophy

It's an open forum at Phyllis', and exhibits give local artists a chance to express themselves to a wide audience.

Rotating exhibits provides change, which is a positive here.

Exhibiting

Make an appointment to present slides or original pieces for review and explain your work. Phyllis' Musical Inn will not accept pieces that might alarm patrons, but flexibility prevails if the artist takes the lead.

Phyllis' Musical Inn works with the artist on installation. One large wall about 25' by 6' is available, and there are a few scattered, smaller spaces. The stage is usable, as is the beer garden during the summer.

Artist is responsible for insurance.

Artwork is purchased by contacting the artist directly. Phyllis' Musical Inn does not take a commission.

Openings can be held, but there are no drink discounts. Artist may bring in food.

Artist receives access to Phyllis' mailing list, and the bar will promote exhibits in its regular *Reader* ads. Inside the bar, the artist may put out flyers and post a price list and bio. Phyllis' Musical Inn will put out a suggestion box so patrons can critique exhibits and the artists can get some feedback.

Printer's Row
American

550 S. Dearborn Street
Chicago, IL 60605
312/461-0780
Lunch: Mon.-Fri., 11:30 a.m.-2:30 p.m.
Dinner: Mon.-Thurs., 5:30 p.m.-10 p.m.; Fri.-Sat., 5:30 p.m.-11 p.m.

Peter Grills, General Manager
3 Months
Wall Hangings

Printer's Row offers a comfortable, clubby atmosphere, rich with dark woods and oversized chairs. Everything, down to the white linen tablecloths, is simple and elegant. The food comes delightfully prepared, often with edible flowers that add both color and flavor.

The restaurant attracts an upscale, professional clientele. Lunch draws a large concentration of businesspeople. Expect to pay $70-90 per couple for dinner. Reservations are recommended and necessary on weekends.

Art Philosophy

Printer's Row exhibits artwork for the charm it brings to the restaurant. Printer's Row tries to patronize Midwestern companies for its food and supplies, and features Midwestern artists in its effort to emphasize the importance of local talent.

Printer's Row often contacts the Art Institute of Chicago to attract artwork. The restaurant seeks realistic, impressionistic pieces.

Exhibiting

Make an appointment to present work for review. Original pieces are preferred.

Artist handles installation. Nails OK. Pieces are displayed in both the bar and dining room.

Artist is responsible for insurance and must sign a waiver.

Artwork is purchased by contacting the artist directly. Printer's Row does not take a commission.

Openings are negotiable.

Artist is responsible for promotion. Inside the restaurant, understated promotion may consist of small title cards placed next to each piece.

The Rainbo Club
Tavern

1150 N. Damen Avenue
Chicago, IL 60622
312/489-5999
Mon.-Fri., 4 p.m.-2 a.m.; Sat., 8 p.m.-3 a.m.; Sun., 8 p.m.-2 a.m.

Dee Taira, Owner
1 Month
Unrestricted

A pink neon sign reading "Rainbo Club" hangs over a desolate exterior. Surprisingly, through a rusty, uninviting screen door is a lively bar with elegant touches.

Attention is immediately drawn to a fantastic old circular stage. Supported by Classical columns and back-lit in pink or blue neon, this is definitely the focal point of the bar. Deeper inside, one notices the beautiful inset wood and glass cabinets that line the wall on either side of the entrance.

An old record player plays new music at the whim of the bartenders, who somehow find time to handle the entertainment as they hurry from one end of the long bar to the other taking orders. The beer menu is a group of twelve bottles lined up on the bar counter. (If one of those bottles should happen to fall...)

The limited standing room around the bar fills up quickly, as do the red leather booths and sinking couches off to the sides. The laid-back crowd is made up mostly of artists and people from the neighborhood.

Art Philosophy

The Rainbo Club exhibits artwork to give neighborhood artists a place to exhibit their work. The club gets a good room as a result of the exhibitions.

Exhibiting

The Rainbo Club requires slides representative of the proposed show for review. Artist can leave them at the bar and wait to be contacted. Group shows OK.

Artist handles installation. The walls will not support much weight, but small nails are OK. The main wall is about 35' long, and there are several other smaller spaces available. Two 6' by 2' display cases hold small objects or framed pieces, and the stage highlights a sculpture or large two-dimensional piece set on an easel.

Artist is responsible for insurance, and is warned about the possibility of smoke damage.

Artwork is purchased by contacting the artist directly. The Rainbo Club does not take a commission.

Openings are informal, with bar life going on as usual. Artist drinks free for the night, usually a Friday.

Artist is responsible for promotion. The bar has no mailing list. Inside the bar, the artist can post his or her name, phone number, bio and price list.

River North Café
Café

750 N. Franklin Street
Chicago, IL 60610
312/642-6633
Mon.-Fri., 8 a.m.-5:30 p.m.; Sat., 11 a.m.-5 p.m.

Robert Bearman, Owner
3 Months
Wall Hangings, Mobiles

This bright, upscale deli is nestled under the Ravenswood El tracks. The interior contains a small number of glass tables and wrought-iron chairs. A variety of fresh soups, salads, sandwiches, coffees, beers and wines is served daily. Breakfast and lunch can be eaten in or taken out. The clientele consists mainly of area businesspeople, including interior designers, gallery owners, artists and photographers. Friday afternoons and evenings draw regular gallery hoppers, and Saturday brings in tourists exploring Chicago's gallery district.

Art Philosophy

River North Café exhibits artwork to color the walls and create an atmosphere ranging from soothing to exciting. Variety keeps the place interesting.

Exhibiting

Make an appointment to present original pieces for review. River North Café works with galleries and unrepresented artists.

Artist handles installation. There are three main spaces, measuring 2' by 10', 3' by 10' and 6' by 10'. The back hallway and bathrooms also are open for hanging pieces. Small nails are OK, but hooks screwed into ceiling beams are preferred. The 10' ceilings also are available for mobiles.

Artist is responsible for insurance.

Artwork is purchased by contacting the artist directly. River North Café does not take a commission.

Openings are negotiable.

River North Café stays out of promotion for fear of saying the wrong thing about the artist's work, but allows the artist to post a description of the exhibit, a price list and bio inside the café.

Roscoe's Tavern
Tavern

3354-56 N. Halsted Street
Chicago, IL 60657
312/281-3355
Sun.-Fri., 2 p.m.-2 a.m.; Sat., 2 p.m.-3 a.m.

Shawn-Laree de St. Aubin, Operations Manager
1 Month-6 Weeks
Wall Hangings

A comfortable environment with few distractions, Roscoe's Tavern is conducive to conversation. The visually pleasing space and relaxed atmosphere attract an upscale, mellow crowd. *Gay Life* calls Roscoe's the "gay yuppie's choice."

Roscoe's decor is traditional and pays close attention to detail. Antiques and other Americana are meticulously displayed on a loft running along the room near the ceiling. A row of dark, private booths sits across the large bar, rich in wood and brass. Clips from classic movies are shown on several video monitors, accompanied by low, contemporary music. In the back, a rustic bar room opens out into a quiet patio filled with trees and iron benches.

Art Philosophy

Roscoe's Tavern exhibits artwork to provide exposure for new artists. The bar also benefits from rotating exhibits, which keep its atmosphere fresh and interesting.

Exhibiting

Make an appointment to present photographs, slides or original pieces for review. Group shows OK.

Roscoe's Tavern handles installation, but the artist may be present. Pieces may be hung on the walls with nails or in the windows from hooks in the ceiling. There are 15-25 scattered spaces available for small pieces.

Artist is responsible for insurance and must sign a waiver.

Artwork is purchased by contacting the artist directly or through Roscoe's if the bar is taking a commission. Commission rates are negotiable.

Openings, held on Wednesdays, are arranged on an individual basis.

Roscoe's Tavern promotes exhibits through its normal advertising in gay newspapers, neighborhood newspapers and the *Reader*. The bar will write a press release if given the information. Inside the bar, the artist may place title cards next to each piece and leave a price list behind the bar.

Savories
Coffee House

1700 N. Wells Street
Chicago, IL 60614
312/951-7638
Mon.-Fri., 7 a.m.-7 p.m.; Sun., 9 a.m.-7 p.m.

Violeta Woodward, Manager
1-3 Months
Wall Hangings

Shopping and snacking go hand in hand at Savories, a general store that happens to be a coffee house. The retail side offers an eclectic range of merchandise, including coffee pots and mugs, wicker baskets, greeting cards, T-shirts, decorative boxes, and other gifts and kitchen accessories.

A large counter area displays a wide selection of coffees, juices, bagels, muffins, cookies, cakes and pies, which can be carried over to small wooden tables scattered in the midst of the goods for sale. Savories is a small place that attracts a mix of neighbors and tourists who want to shop and dine under one roof.

Art Philosophy

Savories exhibits artwork to dress up the store for its clientele.

Exhibiting

Make an appointment to present slides or original pieces for review.

Artist handles installation. Nails OK. There is scattered wall space to accommodate five or six pieces measuring about 2' square.

Artist is responsible for insurance.

Artwork is purchased by contacting the artist directly. Savories does not take a commission.

Openings are negotiable.

Artist is responsible for promotion. Inside the coffee house, the artist can post a bio and price list.

Sheffield's/School Street Café
Tavern/Coffee House

3258 N. Sheffield Avenue/1011 W. School Street
Chicago, IL 60657
312/281-4989
Bar: Sun.-Fri., 2 p.m.-2 a.m.; Sat., 2 p.m.-3 a.m.
Café: Mon.-Tues., 10 a.m.-10 p.m.; Wed.-Thurs. & Sun., 10 a.m.-1 p.m.; Fri.-Sat., 10 a.m.-2 a.m.

Ric Hess, Manager, Sheffield's & Hilary S. Lorenz, Manager, School Street Café
1 Month +
Unrestricted

Sheffield's/School Street Café attempts to please all of the people all of the time. The four-room tavern and coffee house accommodates those who prefer noise and those who choose a more quiet atmosphere. The front bar is a small, angular room with wooden furnishings and a stage. The word Chicago is written behind the bar in large wooden letters. The main bar leads to a summer beer garden and a second stage, lush with trees and furnished with long tables and benches that bring together friends as well as strangers. A pool table stands under a suspended canopy, and the sounds of a strolling saxophonist occasionally fill the air.

The center room at Sheffield's begins the transition from bar to coffee house. Like the front room, it is connected to the beer garden and has a seating area with wooden benches and a bar. There is another pool table, but the bar is the main attraction. It is made of dark wood and fitted in the back with a beautiful copper arch supported by wooden pillars. Jewelry and other objects are displayed inside the counter, under glass. Cappuccino, espresso and coffees are served, which can be brought into two remaining rooms that are small, bright and airy. The last room is divided by a third and final stage, where theater groups, performance artists and acoustic musicians have shows. Thursday night is Poetry Night. Cover for performances is between $3-5.

Art Philosophy

Sheffield's/School Street Café believes that public reaction is important for artists, and that its crowd gives the artist an opportunity to get a response from different points of view. A forum for new local talent, the café is on the artist's side and is willing to try new things. The place is open to provocative art with social imagery because interesting shows bring in interesting people. The café solicits artists through the Chicago Artists Coalition and in publications like the *New Art Examiner*.

Exhibiting

Make an appointment to present slides or a representative original piece for review. In addition to fine art, the café sells practical items like jewelry and accessories. Sheffield's/School Street Café normally hosts group shows.

Installation is discussed and carried out by the artist and café. There is ample wall space for a range of sizes. Sheffield's/School Street Café prefers that pieces be hung from museum hooks on molding around the rooms. Jewelry and other items are displayed in glass-enclosed cases.

Artist is responsible for insurance. Very precious, fragile, or small pieces are discouraged. The café will put glass-enclosed works, like photographs, by the pool table.

Artwork is purchased by contacting the artist directly. Sheffield's/School Street Café takes a 15 percent commission.

Openings are negotiable and may include free or discounted drinks as well as food.

Artist has access to the café's mailing list that includes names from the Chicago Literary Arts Coalition. Sheffield's/School Street Café also may print and distribute 3-month calendars featuring the work of exhibiting artists. Inside the café, the artist may post a bio and price list in a discreet location.

Star Top Café
Eclectic

2748 N. Lincoln Avenue
Chicago, IL 60614
312/281-0997
Tue.-Sun., 6 p.m.-11 p.m. or Midnight

Bill Ammons, Partner
Indefinite
Unrestricted

Loud rock 'n' roll and good, rich food create a dining experience at the Star Top Café. The atmosphere is a wild, dynamic and boisterous mix of patterns, textures, sounds, smells and tastes that indulge the senses.

There is definitely a dry humor to the decor at the Star Top. Ceramic kangaroos and raccoons have run of the place, and a plastic bust of Mr. T greets patrons at the door. The room is filled with small tables covered with metallic tablecloths and surrounded by vibrant, paint-splattered chairs. A subtle Western motif is picked up by a cattle-skin pattern on the walls. Leather couches are grouped in a small alcove by the front window, where an old record player spins rock 'n' roll classics. The music will not be turned down for anyone, but it may be turned up on occasion.

The food is unconventional and inventive, and its richness won't leave anyone hungry. Expect to pay about $60 per couple for dinner. The clientele is mixed, tending toward professionals in their 30s and 40s. A large faction of artists and musicians lends a certain chic credibility.

Art Philosophy

Star Top Café seeks pieces that mean something, not commercial work that merely decorates the space. Rotating the exhibits emphasizes the dynamism of the restaurant.

Exhibiting

It is rare that an artist off the street gets shown at the Star Top, but it is possible. Drop off slides for review, and wait to be contacted should there be any interest. Star Top Café normally hosts group shows by friends of the management.

Artist handles installation. Nails OK. Four large walls are available.

Artist is responsible for insurance.

Artwork is purchased by contacting the artist directly. Star Top Café dos not take a commission.

No formal openings.

Artist is responsible for promotion. No promotional pieces are allowed inside the restaurant. If a patron likes a piece, the Star Top will provide the artist's name and phone number.

Sterch's
Tavern

2238 N. Lincoln Avenue
Chicago, IL 60614
312/281-2653
Sun.-Fri., 3:30 p.m.-2 a.m.; Sat., 3:30 p.m.-3 a.m.

Bob Smerch, Owner
1 Month
Wall Hangings

Sterch's is an historic constant in a changing neighborhood. Surrounded by trendy, modern dance clubs, Sterch's remains a small neighborhood bar with an inviting atmosphere. Inside, one has the sense of being in an old attic, discovering an eclectic collection of memorabilia accumulated during the 17 years of the bar's existence.

Sterch's is comfortable and unpretentious. Two large picture windows invite passers-by into the room filled with a mix of people from the area. Square wooden high-backed booths line the wall parallel to the bar. A juke box and video games offer entertainment and amusement.

Art Philosophy

Sterch's has been exhibiting artwork for more than 17 years as a service to new talent looking for exposure. Most of the artists exhibited at Sterch's are students from Chicago art schools and neighboring cities like Rockford and Woodstock. The shows also add interest to the bar's atmosphere.

Exhibiting

Make an appointment to present slides or original pieces representative of the proposed show for review.

Artist handles installation. Nails OK. Artwork is hung on a long wall across from the bar, measuring 14' by 8'.

Artist is responsible for insurance.

Artwork is purchased by contacting the artist directly. Sterch's does not take a commission.

Openings are negotiable, and can range from beer and chips to champagne and caviar depending on the artist's request.

Artist is responsible for promotion. Inside the bar, the artist may post a price list and bio.

Sweet Home Chicago
Tavern

3270 N. Clark Street
Chicago, IL 60657
312/327-3202
Mon.-Fri., Noon-2 a.m.; Sat., Noon-3 a.m.

Paul Haltiwanger, Co-Owner
2-3 Months
Photographs

Sweet Home Chicago attracts a fun-loving neighborhood crowd of artists, actors and young professionals. The bar is bright and comfortable, with lots of standing room and, for those who prefer sitting, a large raised area near the front picture windows.

Live jazz begins at 5 p.m. on Sunday. There is no cover. During the rest of the week, there's a juke box, video games and good old-fashioned conversation. Sweet Home Chicago also offers a selection of sandwiches and pizzas.

Art Philosophy

Sweet Home Chicago exhibits artwork because its clientele appreciates the rotating shows.

Exhibiting

Make an appointment to present slides or original pieces for review.

Artist handles installation. Work is hung from picture rails. A 20' wall is available across from the bar.

Sweet Home Chicago provides insurance for exhibited artwork.

Artwork is purchased by contacting the artist directly. Sweet Home Chicago does not take a commission, but encourages the artist to pass the savings along to potential customers by lowering prices.

Informal openings are usually scheduled Monday through Wednesday in the early evening. Sweet Home Chicago has worked with distributors to host wine tastings at openings.

Artist is responsible for promotion. Inside the bar, the artist may put title cards next to each piece and leave a phone number at the bar.

The 3rd Coast
Coffee House

1260 N. Dearborn Street
Chicago, IL 60610
312/649-0730
Sun.-Thurs., 7:30 a.m.-Midnight; Fri.-Sat., 7:30 a.m.-1 a.m.

Ike Eichling, Co-Owner
1 Month-6 Weeks
Wall Hangings

The 3rd Coast is a leader in Chicago's coffee house revival. The space is bright and comfortable, conducive to reading or conversation. Literature dealing with politics, social welfare and art fills the entranceway, providing fertile discussion inside the coffee house. The 3rd Coast is divided into two distinct areas, each with its own mood. Tables are crowded close together in the main room, a large, rectangular space buzzing with activity. A smaller room, airy and more intimate, overlooks the main area from a slightly raised vantage point.

The clientele at The 3rd Coast consists of a broad spectrum of Europeans, blue-collar workers, seniors, artists and residents of the upscale Gold Coast. The coffee house offers a full menu, complete with exceptional desserts and an extensive selection of wines and liqueurs. Expect to pay about $20 per couple for dinner.

Art Philosophy

One of the advantages of living in a big city is the opportunity to be exposed to beauty, creativity and new ideas. The 3rd Coast strives to offer these opportunities, in part through rotating art exhibits. Exhibiting artwork offers a fresh and stimulating environment to The 3rd Coast's clientele, which consists mainly of five-days-a-week regulars.

Exhibiting

Make an appointment to present slides or original pieces for review. Two different shows take place simultaneously.

Artist handles installation. Nails OK. The main room accommodates pieces measuring about 3' square, hung between wooden panels. Smaller pieces, often photographs, work best on the upper level.

Artist is responsible for insurance and must sign a waiver.

Artwork is purchased by contacting the artist directly. Artist has the option to replace pieces as they are sold or keep them up for the duration of the show. Commission is negotiable.

Openings are held on the upper level. The 3rd Coast will provide wine, cheese and hors d'oeuvres.

Artist may do a promotional mailing on postcards provided by the coffee house. The 3rd Coast will distribute flyers and reimburse the artist for copying expenses. Inside the coffee house, the artist may post a price list, bio and title cards next to each piece.

The 3rd Coast
Coffee House

888 N. Wabash Avenue
Chicago, IL 60611
312/664-7225
Sun.-Thurs., 7:30 a.m.-Midnight; Fri.-Sat., 7:30 a.m.-1 a.m.

Nancy Scanlan, General Manager
1 Month-6 Weeks
Wall Hangings

The 3rd Coast's second location is smaller than the first (only one room). The menu is the same and the clientele is similar, if only a little younger. The atmosphere is relaxed and casual, making this location an ideal hangout for students and other individuals with leisure time.

In this space, one is immediately struck by the aroma of coffee, lined in big barrels in front of the counter. Tables are loosely scattered around square mirrored posts that rise from the old wooden floor. Windows brighten the room, and outdoor seating is available in the summer.

Art Philosophy

One of the advantages of living in a big city is the opportunity to be exposed to beauty, creativity and new ideas. The 3rd Coast strives to offer these opportunities, in part through rotating art exhibits. Exhibiting artwork offers a fresh and stimulating environment to The 3rd Coast's clientele, which consists mainly of five-days-a-week regulars.

Exhibiting

Make an appointment to present slides or original pieces for review.

Artist handles installation. The room accommodates pieces as large as 3' by 3'. Artist must supply hooks and wire for installation.

Artist is responsible for insurance and must sign a waiver.

Artwork is purchased through The 3rd Coast, which takes a 25 percent commission.

No formal openings.

Artist is responsible for promotion. Inside the coffee house, the artist may post a price list, bio and title cards next to each piece.

Traffic Jam
Dance Club

401 W. Ontario Street
Chicago, IL 60610
312/951-0699
Lower Level: Daily, 5 p.m.-4 a.m.
Upper Level: Thurs.-Sat., 9 p.m.-4 a.m.

Melanie Kallal
6 Weeks
Unrestricted

Traffic Jam is a large renovated loft space with wooden floors, visible supports, and walls of exposed brick and muted mauve. In spite of the modern urban construction, the feel of the place is reminiscent of the 1950s.

The size of Traffic Jam recalls a roller skating rink or a school gymnasium. With lots of people in the casual, friendly atmosphere, Traffic Jam has the feeling of a modern-day sock hop. The club serves hot dogs, peanuts and popcorn, and offers live rock 'n' roll Thursday through Saturday on the upper level. Cover is $5 after 9 p.m. Also on Thursday, a psychic performs on the lower level.

The large screen behind the main bar gives one the sense of being at a drive-in movie. Cars are indeed a big part of the club, and photographs of actual traffic jams are on permanent display.

A sunken area to the left of the main bar contains two pool tables. There are more pool tables upstairs, as well as two Skee Ball games. Traffic Jam is a place for good clean fun.

Art Philosophy

Traffic Jam exhibits artwork to enhance and show support for Chicago's artistic community. The club seeks Chicago artists only, and stages contests through local college art departments. Gallery owners and local artists preside as judges.

Exhibiting

Make an appointment to present works for review. Original pieces are preferred, if convenient. Group shows OK.

Artist handles installation. Nails OK. There is a great deal of scattered wall space, and a large wall in the corridor leading to the main bar. Walls are either exposed brick or mauve-painted plaster.

Artist is responsible for insurance.

Artwork is purchased by contacting the artist directly. Traffic Jam does not take a commission.

Traffic Jam will provide free wine at weekday (no Fridays) openings from 5 p.m.-8 p.m. on the first floor. Artist can bring food.

Artist has access to the bar's 1,000-name mailing list, but must do his or her own mailing. Traffic Jam may promote exhibits in its radio, *Chicago Tribune* and *Reader* advertising. Inside the club, the artist can post a price list and title cards next to each piece.

Trio
Diner

3613 N. Broadway
Chicago, IL 60613
312/348-7337
Daily, 8 a.m.-10 p.m.

Cathy Park
3 Weeks
Wall Hangings

Trio is an upscale diner. The front room maintains the traditional dining counter, but the restaurant adds a special flair in cooking and atmosphere that distinguishes it from its old-fashioned counterpart, and a larger second room offers a more formal dining experience.

The food at Trio is fresh and healthy, with an emphasis on vegetables. The portions are large and the prices are small. Expect to get a huge meal for about $10. Bring your own alcohol if desired. Weekend breakfasts are crowded but worth the wait.

A large neighborhood clientele of artists and businesspeople keeps Trio buzzing. The atmosphere is lively but relaxed, and the arty waitstaff adds to the fun.

Art Philosophy

The owners and employees at Trio are all artists. They know what it is like to be looking for exposure, and are glad to offer wall space to the new artist.

Exhibiting

Make an appointment or just drop in to present original photographs or slides of works in other media for review.

Artist handles installation. Nails are not allowed, but Trio does provide gallery hooks. Artist brings in wire and hangs work at night or during nonpeak hours. Trio's two rooms can accommodate pieces as large as 4' by 5'. There are two long walls and three smaller scattered spaces available.

Artist is responsible for insurance.

Artwork is purchased by contacting the artist directly. Trio does not take a commission.

Trio will arrange openings, but cannot close the restaurant. Trio will provide special food trays to the artist at cost.

Trio prefers to keep promotion low-key. Depending on timing, the restaurant will tag regular advertising with the artist's name. Inside the restaurant, the artist can put price lists on the front counter and title cards next to each piece.

Union
Dance Club

3101 N. Sheffield Avenue
Chicago, IL 60657
312/525-5055
Sun.-Fri., 4 p.m.-2 a.m.; Sat., 4 p.m.-3 a.m.

James Geier, Owner
2-3 Months
Unrestricted

Union may look like a local tavern from the outside, and the name may imply a certain blue-collar feel, but it doesn't take more than a second look to realize this is an upscale, progressive dance club. Inside, all that remains of the bar's proletariat construction are brick walls. All the fixtures are slickly designed, black and metallic. Molded pieces of aluminum fit on poles to make high tables for the raised booths that line the walls. Matching chairs appear more concerned with form than function, but are in fact quite comfortable. Reflected light from continuous videos shimmers on narrow, pointed strips of metal that hang over the dance floor from the ceiling, modern stalagtites. A triangular wall with two small aluminum tables points to a door that leads to the second floor, where there is additional dance space and a pool hall.

Every night, DJs play progressive music at Union. Cover is $4 Friday through Monday. Tuesday, ladies drink free; cover is $5. Wednesday, cover is $2 and beers are 25¢. Thursday, drinks are two for one with a $3 cover. Union's menu includes light entrees and more traditional bar snacks like chicken wings, pastas and salads.

Art Philosophy

Union exhibits artwork to give exposure to young talent and provide innovative work for the enjoyment of its patrons.

Exhibiting

Make an appointment to present slides or original pieces for review.

Artist handles installation. Work is shown on both levels.

Artist is responsible for insurance.

Artwork is purchased by contacting the artist directly. Union does not take a commission.

Openings are negotiable.

Union promotes exhibits in the *Reader, Chicago Magazine* and *Inside Chicago*. Artist has access to the bar's mailing list. Inside the bar, the artist may post a price list, bio and title cards next to each piece.

Urbus Orbis
Coffee House

1934 W. North Avenue
Chicago, IL 60622
312/252-4446
Mon.-Thurs., 11 a.m.-Midnight; Fri.-Sat., 11 a.m.-1 a.m.; Sun., 10 a.m.-10 p.m.

Tom Handley, Owner
Indefinite
Unrestricted

One is immediately struck by the magnitude of Urbus Orbis. Even the oversized tables, decorated with beautiful black renderings of alchemy symbols, seem small in the vast room. White painted brick and two rows of large windows create a bright, airy atmosphere that opens up the room even more, especially during the day.

Dominating the space is a round bar that chronicles the history of the world through a series of removable panels. The bar surrounds an exposed kitchen, where soups, sandwiches, salads, coffees and teas are prepared. No alcohol is served, but it may be brought in. Corkage fee is $1.

Urbus Orbis also offers a Cabaret Room for theater, music and other spoken art. In contrast to the rest of the space, the room is dark, close and smoky. Cover is usually $8-12.

Art Philosophy

Urbus Orbis exhibits artwork as a result of being open to the influences of patrons and employees. The coffee house follows a free format that allows and encourages the exchange of ideas.

Artwork adds to the room and roots the coffee house more firmly in the neighborhood.

Exhibiting

Make an appointment to present slides, working drawings or finished pieces for review. If a piece works in the space, it will be accepted for display. Urbus Orbis exhibits works by various artists at the same time.

Artist handles installation, but the coffee house will provide technical assistance. Nails OK on certain walls. Scattered spots are available between windows in the main room, and there are large open walls in the cabaret.

Artist is responsible for insurance.

Artwork is purchased by contacting the artist directly. Urbus Orbis may take a commission.

Openings are negotiable.

Artist is responsible for promotion. Urbus Orbis will make its mailing list available to the artist. Inside the coffee house, the artist may post a price list, bio and title cards next to each piece.

Vegetaria Restaurant
Vegetarian

3182 N. Clark Street
Chicago, IL 60657
312/549-0808
Mon., 11 a.m.-6 p.m.; Tue.-Sun., 10 a.m.-Midnight

Shaun Murray, Assistant Manager
3 Weeks
Wall Hangings

Owned and operated by vegetarians, Vegetaria Restaurant offers breakfast, lunch and dinner to hard-core herbivores and to people simply seeking some variety in their diets. The room is small and bright, and the atmosphere is friendly. It is a comfortable spot to hang out and enjoy good, healthy and economical food. Any member of the staff will answer questions about diet, nutrition and food combining. Vegan, Lacto-Vegetarian and some Macrobiotic meals are available. Dine in, carry out or call for delivery. Expect to pay $15-20 per couple for dinner.

Art Philosophy

Vegetaria Restaurant exhibits artwork as part of a campaign to stimulate and attract new customers. A changing environment is important for a dynamic clientele. Large windows allow the artwork to be seen from outside, thus generating interest in the restaurant.

Recognizing the difficulty artists face in getting exposure, Vegetaria is happy to offer an opportunity. The restaurant is interested in organic, naturalistic works, often with scientific themes.

Exhibiting

Leave name and number at Vegetaria and wait for a call to arrange a presentation of slides or original pieces for review. Group and themed shows OK.

Installation is handled by the artist and the restaurant. Screws OK.

Artist is responsible for insurance.

Artwork is purchased through Vegetaria, which takes a 25 percent commission.

Openings, held on Monday evenings, are arranged on an individual basis.

Exhibits are promoted on Vegetaria's menu. Vegetaria Restaurant develops small program books for each specific show, and distributes flyers to its mailing list. Exhibit information also is tagged on the restaurant's normal advertising. Inside the restaurant, the artist may post a price list, bio and description of the work.

Wholesome Roc Gallery
Coffee House

2360 N. Clybourn Avenue
Chicago, IL 60614
312/883-8746
Tue.-Thurs., 7 p.m.-Midnight; Fri.-Sat., Noon-Midnight; Sun., Noon-10 p.m.

Simone Bouyer, Owner
1 Month
Unrestricted

Wholesome Roc Gallery is a converted loft that maintains both the layout and atmosphere of a home, complete with a well-worn flight of stairs. One enters an informal sitting area with a small open kitchen slightly to the left, where coffee, espresso, herbal tea, pastries, Freez Pops, nachos, seasonal sandwiches and free peanuts in the shell are served. The space branches off into two additional sections. The front is the site of performances, film screenings and organized discussions. Two rooms comprise the rear half, one containing a table with literature about upcoming activities at Wholesome Roc and other organizations, and a quiet back room with comfortable couches.

Something is always going on at Wholesome Roc--the coffee house is one of the most involved alternative art spaces in Chicago. Near the entrance, a blackboard reads "Ask Us." Good advice. Formal activities include Test Tube Theatre on Tuesday; Muses Channel, a spontaneous musical discovery, on Wednesday; and Film Realm, free films, on Friday. The Poetry Tostada, an Open Mike, is held every third Saturday and Sunday of the month. Stories in Motion, where new works are read and discussed, takes place every second Saturday and Sunday of the month. Sometimes there is a cover of $2-5, but often special events are free.

Art Philosophy

"Is there anywhere in Chicago where any artist can exhibit, perform, screen films and videos simply because they desire to do so?" Yes. Billed as a gallery and museum, Wholesome Roc is dedicated to bringing art closer to the public. Like a museum, the coffee house offers annual memberships ranging from $15-1,000. Members receive 10 percent off art purchases; a free quarterly newsletter, *Planet Roc*; free admission to special events including an annual members party; and a free T-shirt.

Wholesome Roc Gallery exhibits artwork to attract and encourage new local artists. The coffee house asks, "Why suffer to convince a gallery to show your work? Why give huge commissions to gallery owners?"

Exhibiting

Wholesome Roc Gallery does not see much of the work it exhibits before it is installed. Instead, the artist completes a detailed Show Request Form with information about the artist's work and goals. The form also asks for an exhibit resume; the titles, media, dimensions and prices of proposed pieces; and why the artist wants a show. It also is a contract requiring the artist to work at Wholesome Roc for 15 hours a week during the show. Wholesome Roc only hosts group shows.

Artist comes in on the first Tuesday of the month to install the exhibition. Wholesome Roc Gallery will assist if asked. Installation requirements are explained on the Show Request Form. Nails OK. Four rooms are available.

Artist is responsible for insurance and must sign a waiver.

Patrons make offers for pieces on Bid Forms and are contacted by the artist. Wholesome Roc Gallery takes a 30 percent commission.

Artist Receptions are held the first Saturday and Sunday of the month. An artist pot-luck dinner is scheduled and Wholesome Roc also chips in.

Wholesome Roc Gallery prints promotional postcards that are mailed, made available at the coffee house, and given to the artist. Exhibits also are publicized in *Planet Roc*. Inside the coffee house, the artist may post a bio and title cards next to each piece.

Wild Onion
American

3500 N. Lincoln Avenue
Chicago, IL 60657
312/871-5113
Mon.-Thurs., 11:30 a.m.-11 p.m.; Fri.-Sat., 11:30 a.m.-Midnight;
Sun., 10 a.m.-3 p.m. for brunch, 5 p.m.-10 p.m. for dinner.

Tony Mongello, General Manager
3-1/2 Months
Unrestricted

Wild Onion fuses the spaces and colors of Classical Rome and the American Midwest into a cohesive, pleasant experience. The walls appear as elegant frescoes, but may just as easily be described as the color of corn or wheat. Structurally, the scale of the rooms is reminiscent of vaulted Roman baths, while wooden beam supports make more specific references to a loft space or barn. Long, luxurious curtains draped between doorways make the transition from one room to the next as subtle and dramatic as a ceremonial procession. Cattle skulls, hung in the corridor between dining rooms, suggest the passage of livestock on the open range that built the Midwestern economy.

There are three dining areas at the Wild Onion. The casual front room houses a long stretch of booths and tables across from the bar and a separate, raised space for nonsmokers. The rear room, where larger and private parties are served, is elegantly lit and has a presence and formality unlike the other spaces. This is largely a result of its isolation from the other sections and the progression through draped portals which leads one into the space. The most informal part of the restaurant is the raw wood gazebo outside. Wild Onion serves regional American cuisine ranging from fresh, simple sandwiches to elaborate gourmet entrees. Expect to pay between $20-50 per couple for dinner, and enjoy Sunday brunch for about $10 per person.

Art Philosophy

Wild Onion exhibits artwork because it creates a lively and funky atmosphere attractive to a younger clientele.

Exhibiting

Make an appointment to present slides or original pieces for review. Most of the art at Wild Onion comes from August House gallery, but space is reserved for one unrepresented artist during each show.

Artist handles installation. Nails OK. Three walls are available in the main room, one measuring 14' by 10' and two measuring 6' by 10'. Three spaces also are available in the smaller room, two measuring 12' by 10' and one measuring 8' by 10'.

Artist is responsible for insurance.

Artwork is purchased by contacting the artist directly. Wild Onion does not take a commission.

Openings are held on Sundays from 3 p.m.-5 p.m., with appetizers and a cash bar.

Wild Onion and August House gallery each do a mailing to promote exhibits. Inside the restaurant, the artist can post a price list and bio.

The Wrightwood Tap
Tavern

1059 W. Wrightwood Avenue
Chicago, IL 60614
312/549-4949
Sun.-Fri., Noon-2 a.m.; Sat., Noon-3 a.m.

Bob Donohue, Owner
2 Months
Wall Hangings

Small and warm with an amber hue, the Wrightwood Tap is a friendly, comfortable neighborhood bar. Trophies fill shelves and are hung on the walls, acknowledging the prowess of teams sponsored by the bar in baseball, volleyball, darts and other sports. Loud music booms from scattered speakers connected to a juke box with an eclectic range. Video games stand in every corner, and a bowling game is positioned near a row of tables in the back. There are two dart boards, one in the main room and one secluded in a tiny rear space where a book case offers a wide range of reading material.

No food is served at the Wrightwood Tap. Nonalcoholic wines are available.

Art Philosophy

The Wrightwood Tap emphasizes its first and foremost function as a bar, but willingly provides wall space for interested artists. The bar started to exhibit work at a patron's request to use the wall, and continues to do so to support the local artistic community and change the bar's atmosphere.

Exhibiting

Make an appointment to present slides, snapshots or original pieces for review.

Artist handles installation. A 12' by 5' wall is available.

Artist is responsible for insurance.

Artwork is purchased by contacting the artist directly. The Wrightwood Tap does not take a commission.

No formal openings.

Artist is responsible for promotion. Inside the bar, the artist can place title cards next to each piece and post a price list on the wall or leave it at the bar.

Yes!

Consider the following establishment(s) for future editions of
Eat Your Art Out, Chicago:

Name of establishment_____

Street address_____

Phone number_____

Art contact_____

Name of establishment_____

Street address_____

Phone number_____

Art contact_____

I'm interested in additional information about:

_____The bars and restaurants best suited for my artwork

_____Setting up a system for exhibiting art in my bar or restaurant

_____Specific artists that exhibit work in bars and restaurants

Please return with your name and address to:
Eat Your Art Out, Chicago, c/o Urbs In Photo, Inc.,
P.O. Box 06236, Sears Tower, Chicago, IL 60606